Team Building

The Ultimate Guide to Build & Manage Winning Teams

(Quickly Increase Team Building and Project Management Skills for Better Employee Engagement)

Randy Anderson

Published By **Simon Dough**

Randy Anderson

*Team Building: The Ultimate Guide to Build &
Manage Winning Teams (Quickly Increase Team
Building and Project Management Skills for Better
Employee Engagement)*

ISBN   978-1-998901-29-6

Legal & Disclaimer

Table of contents

Table of contents

Chapter 1: What Is Team Building?

Team building is a device which goals at growing teamwork and cooperation inside a piece unit. A agency can only be effective if the people recognize every extraordinary and are stimulated to use their strengths for the purpose of moving closer to their commonplace goal or purpose. Each member of a set has a important role to play, and they may be people who are accountable for the fulfillment of a enterprise corporation. Today's corporations and companies face pretty a few trouble collectively with outsourcing, understaffing, burnout, morale-defeating sports, and so forth. It is in times like people who enterprise proprietors start to recognize how crucial it is to have right conversation within an enterprise organisation. Hence, efforts are being enforced for the cause of nurturing verbal exchange internal a business enterprise.

For a team to be effective, it's miles vital that its individuals want to installation a time for converting their mind and for purchasing acquainted with each other. According to the element of view of an employee, it's far useful to be a part of a set due to the truth this commonly gives her or him a sense of possession and loyalty. In fantastic phrases, group building is all approximately the try to beautify the joint regular standard overall performance of the organization of human beings sharing the identical commonplace purpose. The importance of institution constructing come to be identified and desired thru pretty a few agencies close to the prevent of the 20th century. Sadly, no longer all groups or groups realise the significance of institution constructing; some are though within the dark with regards to this depend. It's just like a indistinct idea which people think is worthy, but they do not truely recognize it or offer any credibility to it.

To recognize what group building is all about, one has to delve deeper into the idea behind group building and be clean about the which means that of businesses inside the first area. Most people frequently companion the word 'group' with a collection of people. However, this isn't always the real this means that of a team. Not all groups of humans are groups, first-class those who share a not unusual goal are a group. However, virtually having a not unusual intention is not sufficient to bind the group together or to make it a successful one. The individuals of a team want to usually be inclined to put in their extraordinary efforts, and to modify with the others and paintings collectively accurately to make a a success organization. If the people have terrible relationships with each special, then the overall achievement of the crew could be limited.

When it involves crew building, the institution must typically encompass the mission of continuously monitoring their improvement and enhancing their performances in order that the organization's not unusual overall performance may be greater. Also, all the restricting or inhibiting elements must be removed. One have to try out taken into consideration certainly one of a kind strategies to organization building and spot what works quality for all the people of the organization.

Team Building Basics

By the quit of the 20th Century, companies everywhere inside the worldwide had commenced out to understand the importance of teamwork in an corporation enterprise's capability to offer pleasant offerings and continue to be competitive. That stated, even within the twenty first Century, the term 'crew building' seems notably vague and often used out of context. It isn't always very clean to define the term 'crew'. Even so, the first-rate definition is that a set consists of a set of folks who unite to benefit a particular purpose. Thus, people who are a part of a fixed need no longer belong to a collection, notwithstanding the truth that those who belong to a team are contributors of the business enterprise. Typically, human beings going for walks collectively in companies face a few issues. Some of these problems encompass:

- Confusion of goal

- Difficulty seeing every other's perspectives

- Lack of enthusiasm

- Lack of faith

- Personality Conflicts

Building businesses is the technique in which the ones issues are ironed out simply so the group of humans can end up a 'team' and paintings collectively for the success of desires. Experts agree that every enterprise is going through a few methods earlier than it becomes a group, even though these strategies may not be obvious on the time. These tactics are:

- Forming - the earliest degree of agency introduction

- Storming - humans inside the organization warfare to set up their identities

- Norming - group individuals accumulate properly-set up positions within the crew

- Performing - the organisation has emerge as a professional organization

These programs assist crew formation inside the following techniques:

- It speeds up crew formation thru demanding situations which is probably designed to help group individuals examine the values of teamwork

- It is as a substitute strategic in nature

- It makes a speciality of developing the abilities, mind-set and behaviors critical for real teamwork

When is group constructing maximum successful? Exercises are regularly undertaken in-house. Sometimes, it's far outsourced to experts. Regardless of who handles the packages, powerful factors are essential to make group constructing physical games a roaring achievement. Let's discover those factors:

- Relevant - Team constructing sports activities have to have a particular reason.

6

- Precise - Exercises have to lease precise system which might be taken again to the place of work to reinforce the crew spirit

- Commitment - Programs want to be linked to awesome professional improvement efforts. Follow-up and feedback are scheduled on the stop of this system to assess the effectiveness and ensure continued benefits.

- Experience - The facilitator has sufficient expertise approximately the company further to group building and, consequently, permits individuals to get the maximum from this device.

To make certain that group constructing applications are a fulfillment and to maximise their effect, it is vital to combine the 4 P's into crew constructing programs:

- Personalize - to healthy the dreams of individuals

- **Program** - to ensure extended-term behavioral trade

- **Participate** - to ensure that everybody blessings from this device

- **Practical** - to offer system that group contributors can art work with even after this gadget

A group consists of a set of humans walking together to accumulate a not unusual intention. Team constructing programs redesign a set of human beings into an inexperienced, successful organization. Even mounted, a achievement agencies have to be exposed to crew constructing sports so you can maintain with the harmonious operating courting and take it to more heights.

Team Building Tips

Learning to construct a sturdy, dynamic institution takes a whole lot of hard artwork. After loads trial and errors, you will analyze what works in employer building and what does now not paintings. Sometimes we studies the hard manner. My guidelines for constructing a sturdy team are listed under:

Know your function

As a group member, we can not all be superstars. There are key position players that make up every and each a achievement organization. For example, everybody has heard of Peyton Manning, right? The longtime Colts quarterback now with the Broncos? Do you recognise who his preferred receiver is? Do you recognize who his favored receiver become? Do you recognize the center's name that snaps him the ball? Do you understand the names of any of the offensive lineman on his modern-day-day organization? Probably now not. However, with out those function game enthusiasts, there may be no team. Do your characteristic on your team? At the administrative center, do you recognise what is anticipated of you?

Communicate

In my opinion, communication is the most vital problem in institution building. Why? Are you a thoughts-reader? Can you expect what your manager or worker is thinking? You apprehend what occurs at the same time as we ASSUME? You make an A__ out of U and ME. Have you ever been involved in a non-public dating and there has been a communication breakdown? We all have in some unspecified time inside the destiny. When we get off beam, it is normally because of a lack of communication. After all, if you have no choice to talk together together with your business enterprise people or cherished ones, it is time to find out a new institution.

Know your holiday spot

All too regularly I listen co-personnel, institution people, employees or maybe managers say a few difficulty like "I don't know why we are even doing this, it is now not going to help." Does your group even recognize why they arrive to the administrative center early every day? Do they even recognize why they live late? Knowing your excursion spot includes quick-time period and lengthy-term dreams. Keep the ones at the vanguard of all of us's thoughts. If anybody is aware of the WHY, they'll decide out the HOW.

Reevaluate periodically

Just like my former teach at halftime who stated, "The excellent companies are those that could adjust midway thru the game," being able to regulate and make modifications at the fly is essential. I'm a business enterprise believer in adaptability. When your group faces an sudden impediment or cut-off date, how are you going to react? After all, existence will throw you a curveball; it is inevitable. It's how we react to the curveball that counts.

Put the Team first

Putting the institution first approach putting your self 2nd. If it benefits the institution more by using doing a wonderful venture, then that desires to be the rule of thumb of thumb. You might not see the private advantages initially, however in case you located the team's fine pastimes in advance than your very private, the crew will move masses in addition, quicker.

Don't Quit

Have you ever desired to save you a few problem on your life? Sure. We all have. Here's what I actually have observed: after you succumb to quitting, it will become easier and less difficult. You do not need that mentality. But fulfillment works the same way. Once you learn how to make it art work, it becomes a addiction which gets simpler and less complicated. You do need that mentality. Surrounding yourself with a extraordinarily useful group will take you to new ranges.

Role of a Team Leader

To be a very good leader, you should apprehend your function and have the self guarantee of your group individuals. Your organization members want to look as a lot as you and rely upon you to influence them to success. Remember, properly leaders are decided thru mainly due to the truth humans take delivery of as proper with and admire them, in place of the technical capabilities they very own. Jesus Christ, Prophet Muhammad, Gautam Buddha and Mahavira have been first rate leaders due to the fact their lovers had entire self belief in their control trends. For a set to artwork nicely, it desires an in a characteristic individual to manual. The wonderful institution participant isn't continuously the brilliant chief, and the terrific chief want not to be the best participant on a group. Know and understand your strengths and weaknesses. Once you know what your strengths and weaknesses are, you may construct the splendid possible businesses spherical you. The following are all key additives to the role a fixed chief plays:

• Know and recognize your targets and the manner to accumulate them. You need to realise why the institution fashioned. Accordingly, you may plan the way to transport about accomplishing that purpose.

• Build a nicely-balanced institution. To satisfy the organization's aim, each member need to supplement each exclusive. You want one-of-a-kind individuals who're robust in numerous matters. Diversity subjects.

• Get the awesome from each group member. You have so as to inspire your participants and inspire them to strive their tremendous. Make each member at the crew enjoy similarly vital. Every member of a crew is crucial. He or she has a specific characteristic to play in the organization and what she or he does is in addition critical inside the direction of reaching the purpose.

• Instill superb strength. If you found truly, your organization will expect absolutely. When given a mission, do now not see what you cannot do; art work in step with what you may do. It is tremendous electricity that helped India win the Twenty20 Cricket World Cup in 2007. They believed they may win, and they did.

• Communicate. You can not be a leader if you lack the important verbal exchange talents required for the location of team leader. You should normally be prepared to talk with others in your institution and be inclined and able to assist your organisation with conflict selection.

• Lead thru example. If the leader does not observe the guidelines that she or he units for the crew, the crew will in no manner be added approximately. When your agency contributors see you giving a hundred percent, they too will observe. It may not arise right away, but it'll appear.

• Praise! When the team succeeds, an wonderful chief will usually reward the group, but at the same time as it fails, the chief will take obligation. Those who perform particularly well want to be congratulated within the the front of all. If someone inside the institution is beneath-appearing, you want to take the man or woman apart and talk with the member. Never have a personal communicate with someone in the presence of others, specifically if the dialogue consists of bad feedback.

• Make selections bravely and boldly. A well leader will make formidable choices and maintain on with them. Sometimes, they will no longer work, but most usually they'll be proper alternatives. Don't be afraid to fail at the equal time as making picks. Remember, try all over again.

• Be inclined to confess you're wrong. Humility is a critical amazing. If, as a leader, you have got made a incorrect desire, do not enjoy horrible to confess it. We all make mistakes once in a while. Learn from it. Let your disasters propel you to do higher within the future. Your group will apprehend you for admitting your faults.

• Encourage your individuals to revel in themselves. The organization need to experience what they're doing. If someone to your group isn't always cushty, discover what the problem is. Sometimes, all you want to do is alternate the member's responsibilities, or possibly even attitude about the desires and dreams of the group building and how that particular group member is a cost contribution to the institution.

Characteristics of a High-Performance Team

If we are going to spend time on foot on a collection, we would really like it to be profitable. Most folks would really like it to be a 'immoderate-overall performance group', and we might all want to enjoy we're a part of the motive it's miles excessive performance. To get began out out on that route, proper right here are the 2 characteristics of a high-overall performance group:

Trust

You may additionally moreover feel this is obvious, however it isn't. Trust is continually tough to set up, and smooth to lose. On a set, everybody ought to realize that they may be supported and valued by means of way of way of each other and that human beings maintain their phrase and do not damage it. It's hard to remember someone who could not maintain their word even as they're pronouncing they'll do a little element. There want to be have a look at-thru to installation take into account. If virtually all people discovers an errors or hassle of their work, they have to convey it in advance so all organization participants can assist discover an answer and sense protected. This develops a revel in of personal dedication to every great and the institution as a whole.

Respect

One of the proper techniques to illustrate apprehend is to pay hobby for facts. When others on the organization communicate, it is respectful to pay attention patiently and wait until they give up after which ask questions for expertise. Anyone at the institution can carry up additional problems or mind to assist whole the trouble, and in a respectful environment, they need to experience comfortable doing so. The group must extend ideas and plan picks together. Anyone who acknowledges that a person has now not had a threat to contribute to a discussion must ask them for their take on the state of affairs. Normally, each member of the organization may additionally have some unique enjoy, skills, or information this is desired. The aggregate can be superb for every crew member and each furthermore recognizes and appreciates what the other employer individuals deliver that they do now not.

When someone on the institution disagrees, you want to look at why and if there is a case to be made. The debate isn't only endorsed, however moreover required for maximum topics. Even whilst it seems there was smooth agreement, it makes enjoy to ask if there can be an opposing perspective, and if so, what would it be? Someone on the group may additionally say, "This appeared too easy, what have we unnoticed?" "Is there a few element that would come out and chunk us later? What else are we able to maintain in mind?" Building on each superb's mind produces unified group choices and answers. No one character need to take complete credit score rating score for locating a solution. Team people must recognise they will be all more powerful working together than they ever can be running aside. It's not unusual for scientists and researchers to touch upon their work about how the whole lot they accomplish is on the shoulders of others who had come earlier than or made tips.

Chapter 2: Creating Successful Teams With Team Building

Are you seeking to create new thoughts, a success strategies, and a beneficial method to a rougher monetary surroundings? Hoping to beautify and decorate your group`s communique, collaboration and cooperation? Do you need to offer your personnel with the hottest, maximum contemporary strategies and gear for success on the equal time as supplying up encouragement and concept in some unspecified time in the future of the ones trying instances? If you replied sure, then it's far proper that you're reading this e-book because group building is for you! As mentioned formerly, group building is the technique of exploring how a group (or groups) of humans art work collectively. It evokes a group tactic for efficaciously operating on an assignment or venture. It may be a dependent scenario or a miles much less formal get together. By manner of coordinated sports activities sports, sports and responsibilities, a superb institution building enjoy will deliver human beings collectively as a cohesive organization. And with the very last reason of developing communications, productiveness, improvement, and know-how, organisation building encourages no longer only corporation development but individual improvement as nicely.

The sports activities and responsibilities embody an hobby, sport or amusement with each organization member taking on particular roles inside the course of the institution constructing enjoy. The involvement of every and every group member, as well as their talents and techniques, are tested. One of the biggest blessings (along issue strengthening and growing a a hit and unbeatable organization) is being able to apprehend the capabilities and talents of your group and matching them at the side of your organisation's wishes and requirements. At the middle, organization constructing is handiest a organisation of humans studying one another and spending some excellent time together. Life is so busy and often we now not frequently have the opportunity to actually (and I suggest without a doubt) get to recognize our paintings friends. And would not we all art work a chunk more efficiently and successfully if we were advocated to discover extra about the people (and their capabilities) we paintings with?

By utilising a hard and fast building enjoy, with a specific motive and finale, an company empowers the crew at the same time as on the equal time presenting the possibility to recognize what makes a winning organization. As a stop end result, you'll amplify valuable conversation and normal overall performance skills, tweak and enhance body of people relationships, be higher capable of encourage and inspire staff to do their outstanding art work and display them that the corporation is invested and does care. Empowering humans by way of way of manner of manner of company building is a win-win scenario. It allows an commercial organisation business enterprise to offer the knowledge and system for actually everyone from the fits to the the the front line (and all people in among) to understand every different, be inspired, work collectively and be the extraordinary they'll be.

Learn How to Manage Your Team

Team constructing sports activities are a pinnacle tool in analyzing the manner to govern a collection. But, they'll be greater than only a tool. I surprise how an entire lot of us save you to realize that we spend extra time with the humans at paintings than we do with our husbands, better halves, children, buddies, and one-of-a-kind own family individuals. For the maximum detail, we understand very little approximately our co-humans. We have to compromise with, remedy problems with, talk with, take course from, associate with, and get at the aspect of them each day.

When considering powerful institution building activities and the manner to manipulate a group, the manager has to glance through the eyes of the personnel. Why? Because the employee could be doing all of the obligations the supervisor assigns. Through their behavior, an worker will make or ruin a group. They should see the gain of any crew building hobby. Then, they need to accept as true with they'll use the instructions they have got been taught. They have to buy into the thoughts the group constructing sports activities have established to be nicely simply really worth converting their behavior for.

Effective group building activities and identifying the way to manage a group starts offevolved offevolved with the supervisor locating out if those they are coping with see things the same manner. The first-class fulfillment will occur at the same time as personnel experience like they may be protected in making topics better. The manager must share his or her imaginative and prescient for the organization building interest and be prepared to answer any questions about it. Answering questions are what makes the worker's experience stable and cushty to pursue the interest. After an powerful session (or series of durations), the manager have to be capable of control individuals who can paintings properly together. Problems ought to be decreased. Everyone have to revel in higher approximately coming to art work every day. (This is in that you smile and agree.)

As an employee, what do group building sports activities mean? Are they critical? Are they beneficial? Are they a waste of time? Or, do they assist make going to artwork every day a better region than it come to be in advance than? That is the critical element. The place of job wishes to be a better vicinity than it have become earlier than. That is the aim that each supervisor must be walking in the direction of. Picking sports that make it well well worth the time some distance from the administrative center is vital if the manager desires to have a better group than in advance than the sports activities activities.

The various set of institution building gear that managers must pick out from makes it feasible to develop teamwork. The intention is to improve how people paintings collectively from three hundred and sixty 5 days to one year. At the very least, the questions suggested right right here want to be spoke back as a part of the training while selecting team building sports activities. Two essential benefits come from deciding on the proper sports that promote teamwork. The first one is higher activity everyday overall performance, however the most crucial one isn't always having to control performance problems month after month.

The Advantages of an Escape Game

A collection of group constructing business enterprise sports are available for folks that work relentlessly for the goodwill of the company. Games are available in classes as numerous as puzzles, mysteries, adventure, traditional, escape, and spying. Each of the video video games in an get away room comes with a very precise tale and masses of worrying conditions. Each of the game calls for a set of -8 people to tide over demanding situations and emerge triumphantly. Every member of the organization has to play with specific suggestions to acquire the victory. Winning and losing might rely on the collective ordinary typical performance of the group, never on a single member. Furthermore, the actual motive of an break out room is to inspire the enjoy of crew building and bonding the numerous gamers of a group. The members take a seat together aspect by means of element, play collectively, scream together and inside the device, pass at once to realise the shared aim of eking out a win. In the route of gambling the sport, a stage of remember develops due to the fact the contributors must rely upon every different for the preferred end result.

Every member of the institution want to give their great and art work difficult to the very surrender of a group constructing interest and stay committed. Dedication like that's what employers desperately search for in their personnel, and the cause institution building is becoming popular. For an enterprise, the price involved might be very trifle in assessment to the blessings to be had with group building video games. As a end result, a growing significant type of company houses are making an funding the cash in which the circulate once more is the most. Team constructing activities together with a manner game like break out-mode lessen the chance of employee turnover. Let's face it, it gets vintage actual rapid having to lease, fireplace and rehire on repeat.

With such a number of advantages related to an get away mission, there can be no wonder why a majority of companies determine on escape room over other alternatives. It's critical to select the proper crew constructing interest choice from the pool of team constructing enterprise sports activities sports. Room Raider is a renowned call inside the location of sharing information about break out video games. Currently dwelling in

Singapore, Room Raider's time table consists of a commonplace go to to places wherein video games are carried out for the reason of fun and group constructing. He has extensive experience within the market and publications organizations regarding the proper holiday spot for a team day out or hobby.

A New Trend in Team Building

The enterprise company practice of a giving over again to the network has been gaining numerous reputation with human beings like Warren Buffet and Bill Gates popping out strongly for such practices. However, in lots of groups, a big majority of employees watch those practices from the sidelines. They are honestly not given a threat to be a part of the organization social responsibility. Corporate social duty (CSR) is a lot greater than philanthropy because it makes a speciality of suitable manage of the economic, social and environmental results of the activities of the company at the place of work, the marketplace, the customers, supply chain, and the network as an entire. However, within the years following the recession, CSR has grown in a large manner; masses simply so many agencies are purposely reversing cutting-edge tendencies wherein philanthropy is deemed as the distinctiveness of the humans who have the very last say. There are many motives for this volte-face.

Many companies were faced with layoffs, dwindling earnings margins and shrinking budgets. Team building sports are pretty expensive. Grappling with a inclined financial outlook, it's far difficult to cough up a low rate variety occasion that could engage, entertain and train personnel. When a organisation spends cash that mixes education with charity, they may optimize their use of the finances. By combining CSR with developmental and schooling goals, companies get a threat to check more packing containers off their listing of priorities!

Many businesses are deeply aware of their social obligations and sense the need to demonstrate this recognition to personnel similarly to offer them a hazard to do a little thing to assist. As a give up result, many businesses for the time being are beginning to keep network-primarily based, beneficial resource-based definitely completely crew building activities for his or her employees in order that personnel get an opportunity to illustrate their experience of social responsibility. Charity events are gaining greater popularity over sports such as taking attendees to the mountains for mountain climbing and so on. Some elements need to be operational to make charity activities gain the whole thing they need to.

The motive that is decided on with the resource of using the commercial enterprise business enterprise have to inspire sturdy vibes in crew people, or have to, at least, be in step with the organizational manner of life. Fortunately, there are masses of packages to select from, and employers might also additionally effortlessly find the occasion that personnel apprehend. The event must include all of the attendees and encourage them to interact meaningfully inside the interest rather than sitting and watching from the sidelines. No spectators allowed at group building activities. Everyone ought to participate in the hobby. The event will now not simplest help the community but might also even decorate the morale of participants and forge a sturdy bond among them. The occasion need to enjoy profitable so that the hobby will become a lifestyles enriching revel in that leaves an effect for an extended period. Therefore, as an opportunity of selecting a clean schooling choice, managers need to permit attendees a hazard to art work with real clients on responsibilities that make a distinction.

CSR company social duty group building occasions could range from planting timber to exploring inexperienced adventure options, recycling, green tips, carpooling thoughts and so forth. It's all approximately teamwork irrespective of the event or interest. So, the following time you're having your industrial organisation corporation conduct a crew constructing event makes nice it is an event that could make a difference to the organization further to the community.

Three Employee Benefits from Team Building

I've already noted numerous benefits from team constructing in this e-book so far, but I even have no longer began to talk about the crucial issue advantages of group constructing. Team building is an vital interest for any enterprise employer or corporation, but it is regularly omitted. If you want to enhance the efficiency interior a business employer enterprise further to the general everyday surroundings of the walking environment, then test the pinnacle 3 key motives team building is so powerful:

Improved Commitment

One of the maximum obvious blessings of group building is the reality that it appreciably improves willpower to each the corporation and the opportunity personnel. Working together creates a rapport and a shared purpose that brings humans collectively, which in flip will decorate the bond personnel sense for the organization. Not satisfactory can you operate organization sports as a way to deliver people together, however it also is a super way to have fun fulfillment as a corporation. Seeing fulfillment rewarded will show employees that there may be a wonderful deal to be received with the resource of walking to the first-rate of their potential and striving to attain desires, so you can improve their strength of mind and motivation in the course of each the organization and their employees.

Improved Communication

We all understand that correct communique is vital inside a enterprise company; most humans can consider several sports in which crossed wires or misconstrued messages have added about havoc inside the place of job. Team building can appreciably enhance communications among employees in your corporation because it makes a speciality of developing the way anyone interacts in addition to how they advise mind and put into effect their abilties. Communication strategies may be labored on in masses of agency activities and hundreds of considered one of a kind types of communication together with electronic mail, cellphone conversations or discussions in individual.

Improved Collaboration

Another important feature of any administrative center is the idea that employees want to be able to paintings collectively with out difficulty and efficaciously without any stress or disruption (this consists of needless drama). Team constructing can draw people collectively in a manner that the everyday walking environment truely can not do. Increased collaboration can bring about a enjoy of achievement that everyone can proportion in. Tasks become less complex and further amusing at the same time as employees come collectively to percent expertise, talk precise options and get critical comments. Being capable of understand tremendous human beings's opinions is an important part of jogging lifestyles, and coming collectively to perform a purpose is worthwhile and powerful on every a personal degree and concerning the agency.

Chapter 3: Why Team Building Games Fail

Some of the principle reasons why crew constructing games fail are as follows:

No information of very last dreams and dreams

Many employers need to spring a surprise on their personnel, but this will be counterproductive. When participants do now not understand the quit dreams, there might be critically hostility between them. Instead, organizations want to tell the crew individuals of the crew building utility. In fact, agencies can skip one step similarly and supply group people the power to select. By respecting the crew's views and choices on the hassle and thru giving them what they want, groups take the first step in the direction of effective team building.

Trying to scare personnel into being a fixed

Facilitators every so often push an considerable challenge for the personnel due to the fact the very first interest. Quite glaringly, this makes more than 90% of the individuals hold lower lower back from giving their first-rate. Facilitators need to design video video games just so there's the right sequencing of sports starting with video video games that deal with the organization's modern-day u . S . Of being. Do the organization members understand each excellent properly? Is there a battle that need to be resolved before the team can paintings as one? The diploma of complexity need to pass up slowly to ensure that everyone can contribute evenly.

Stiff Competition and Rivalry

Competition isn't the idea for teamwork; cooperation is. According to analyze, greater than 87% of times, the greater benefit goes to corporations that took the cooperative method in preference to the competitive one. The motives aren't difficult to discover. When you try to make one institution (or crew member) win, all and sundry loses. If human beings get a experience that they have been now not real enough, it lowers their regular overall performance. Often, competition uncovers the internal jerk in the human beings and some people can also moreover even try unfair manner on the way to win. Besides, people look at a whole lot lots much less whilst they're stopping in competition to each extraordinary. Therefore, team constructing video games need to awareness on providing education in choice to locating and profitable winners.

Lack of strength of will

Sometimes, manipulate makes the error of thinking about this device an exercising in futility; some aspect this is accomplished to hold the employees in accurate humor. This feeling gets conveyed to companies automatically, and results are unsatisfactory. Team constructing is a fee mission, and there need to be a notion on the first-class degree that the company flourishes on the way of existence of team spirit.

Working with the Wrong Consultant

Finally, the exceptional of organisation building video video games is most effective as genuine due to the fact the best of the team building Event Company you are strolling with. Experts internal the problem have the technical skills to guide control in selecting the exceptional sports for their desires. When searching out a set building representative, it is critical to find out a person who is obsessed on what they do and are prepared to artwork with you for the success of your group. If the consultant isn't always as knowledgeable approximately enterprise constructing activities as you need him or her to be, or the representative tries to influence you to decide into buying the maximum pricey team building hobby speedy, then circulate at once to contacting others as an alternative.

Dealing with Conflict

Effective communique consists of choosing the right phrases to deliver our message with the ideal tone and frame language. In many conditions, what want to without problems be diffused turns into infected because of the fact our communication message is misinterpreted (our receiver's belief of the message differs from our rationale). This ebook affords communication strategies to decorate effectiveness in struggle conditions.

There are three components to the conversation message cycle: transmit, gain, and respond. When dealing with war, we need to apply an assertive responsive technique to make certain effectiveness at each step of the cycle. Consider the subsequent techniques for effective communique and resolving conflicts:

• Use "I" statements in vicinity of "you" to reduce emotions of defensiveness or blame by means of using the receiver

• Explain your notion of the scenario and actively invite the receiver to provide an cause for his

• Ask the receiver to perceive if there's a conduct you need to modify to help a splendid cease result and emerge as aware of to the receiver any behaviors she desires to adjust to assist a very precise give up result

• Deal with situations proper away as opposed to hoping they'll go away

• Find a independent place to have your conversation on the identical time as feasible (i.E., far from others, at the same time as each the transmitter and receiver have a immoderate readiness to engage in speak)

• Establish credibility thru regular, assertive behaviors (i.E., you are not aggressive in a unmarried state of affairs, but you're in a few different, so receivers do not realize what to expect from you)

•   Assume others are inclined to find a win-win answer

•   Deal with troubles in vicinity of personalities

•   Recognize specific personalities and be inclined to conform yours to satisfy theirs (now not all people is skilled in sharing their emotions, so you want to attract them out via wondering strategies)

•   Recognize not all people is professional in controlling their emotions so avoid the temptation to allow your emotions to take over

•   Demonstrate receive as actual with and understand to others and expect the equal in move again

•   Be expertise

•   Use a professional mediator to resource in case you aren't able to acquire a fantastic result.

Conflicts are a part of our interpersonal relationships. High performing team individuals are professional in assertive-responsive communication, and groups use healthful war to energize, permit new mind, amplify skills and heighten performance.

The following is an instance of a struggle:

"I pay hobby you've got been gossiping within the lower back of my returned, and I want you to prevent!" The receiver is probably to accumulate your message interpreting a extra competitive tone and feeling defensive due to "you" statements and a loss of possibility supplied to percent his point of view. He have to pick to answer for your statement, or his response can be in addition competitive. Based on his communique fashion, he may moreover close down (stonewalling). This prevents very last contact of the cycle and can bring about harm emotions and misinterpretations, each of which make contributions to decreasing interpersonal and institution morale.

A more powerful declaration makes use of the assertive-responsive technique: "I recognize that you may were pronouncing topics approximately me to others. Is that authentic? Because if there may be a few difficulty I am doing or pronouncing that you do now not recognize, I would like to understand so we will deal with it and find out a manageable answer." In the use of a statement which encompass this, you have got included assertive-responsive communication in the following strategies:

• Assertive communique techniques

• Expressing your feelings in a wholesome manner

• Defining conduct alternate you would really like to look in the exclusive character

• Responsive communique techniques

• Seeking records approximately the alternative trouble of view, which incorporates information and feelings

By the usage of assertive-responsive verbal exchange (terms) with open body language and a super tone you transmit your message (the first step within the verbal exchange cycle) in a manner, which allows the receiver definitely to get maintain of the message as you supposed (step in the conversation cycle). A -manner communicate with perception assessments and questions (step three in the conversation cycle) results. Your purpose in conflict choice is to apprehend the problem and find a answer. It's vital to have a look at that conflict in and of itself is not a awful element. Conflict is a everyday and inevitable a part of life. But you may use conflicts to learn how to locate solutions and propel you earlier to be a higher communicator or even worker.

Chapter 4: Team-Building And Its Objectives.

Developing excessive-performing groups advantages the commercial enterprise, its clients, the teams, and all institution individuals in any corporation. To gain fulfillment with institution-constructing, it's far crucial to preserve a laser-like focus on the goals and desires and the advantages of group-constructing for that specific corporation or administrative center.

The Overarching Goals.

Some don't forget this is about venture frivolous video video video games or indulging in steeply-priced and unnecessary extracurricular sports. Managers and company folks that get hold of as proper with this will right away discard the perception as a whole waste of money and time.

Others who face workplace problems consisting of institution struggle, horrible performance, or unmotivated employees may additionally moreover view crew-constructing as a appropriate however unrealistic purpose. They lack a corporation maintain near on team improvement or the crucial function of control in getting a immoderate regular typical overall performance.

Team development is a PROCESS that takes place over the years. The technique starts offevolved with a group of humans, two or greater, and a pacesetter. The very last cease end result of the approach is a immoderate-acting organization this is particularly stimulated to enhance their overall performance, has properly-advanced techniques and systems for organizing their workload, and derives big delight from their shared accomplishments.

The everyday dreams are to achieve this degree of general performance and make bigger the company via many stages of improvement until it reaches this stage. However, there are wonderful procedures or stages, every with specific dreams and purposes like with each different system. Concentrating on the RIGHT dreams at every step and improving them as you progress will let you in reaching excessive typical overall performance.

The Stage One Objectives.

The Forming degree of group formation has very unique aims and capabilities. These desires MUST be met for the group to improvement to the subsequent level. The group leader's duty is to guarantee that the desires are met.

The Forming degree's goals are as follows:

1. To bind the organization to learn how to realize every other and growth a revel in of agency. Team-building sports activities sports will help in tying them collectively proper now.

2. To align them with their commonplace cause, goals, and goals

46

three. To construct a effective organization way of existence, which encompass shared views, values, and behavioral standards.

4. To outline the leader's function

The Second Stage's Objectives.

While some of the preliminary desires can be carried in advance to this stage, new desires can be created to collect the team further. This diploma is referred to as the Storming diploma, and it is in the course of this degree, contributors can also task their shared cause, management, or social requirements.

The goals at this diploma are as follows:

1. To preserve them centered on their challenge and targets

2. To foster best going for walks connections among all members with the useful resource

of revealing them to important group individuals.

3. To foster collaborative problem fixing and the generation of latest ideas.

four. To set up procedures that art work effectively collectively with each different, which consist of day by day huddles,

flash difficulty solving meetings, ordinary state of play conferences, and communique systems.

5. To define specific brief-term dreams and techniques for commemorating accomplishments and milestones

The Third Stage's Objectives.

After completing the Storming degree, the group might also have grown closer and developed a robust feeling of dedication to carrying out their shared aim. This is known as the Norming degree, and it occurs after they work effectively collectively and feature proper techniques and structures in region.

To fortify the squad to the subsequent degree, the emphasis shifts.

Only a small percent of companies gain the fourth diploma, the immoderate-performing crew. Generally, that is due to the truth they come to be trapped within the Norming diploma. To propel the group beforehand, the reason now's to shift the focal point substantially.

To date, the underlying philosophy has been that there is no 'I' inside the institution. The concept is to supply the business enterprise collectively to carry out their common goals. The motive now might be to reintroduce the 'I'm into the Team, to hold it collectively and foster character greatness and specialization.

At this level, the goals are as follows:

1. To extend commercial enterprise statistics, permitting the team and man or woman contributors to assume expanded duty.

2. To foster creativity, innovation, and management in the context of precise obligations or duties. The leader delegated authority to the group or smaller task companies.

three. To adapt or trade strategies for them to count on extended duty. Team conferences are reduced even as enterprise task businesses are superior. Rotate control of tasks or conferences.

4. To inspire the group to establish its dreams.

With this crystallization of team improvement targets, you can have a much higher risk of efficaciously developing your group.

What Characteristics Define a Winning Team?

How do you build a successful organization or, in the corporation worldwide, a a achievement business employer?

The solution is easy: hold a excellent thoughts-set and growth a winning plan! While executives and presidents are responsible for method, team builders and bosses preserve a effective team spirit.

Positive thinking and group-constructing are effective motivators for eliciting the finest common performance from employees and keeping them glad. Also, group human beings must receive as true with in each their team or corporation and the directive. They need to have confidence in their managerial group and their fellow human beings, keeping in mind that everyone is running within the course of the equal motive.

Team-building Elements.

How do you set up an influential team-constructing event that contributes to the team's togetherness and common performance?

The primary factors are: the event want to be a laugh, even a laugh (there may be no law requiring art work to be a depressing, humorless area); the meeting want to teach some factor treasured and speak the lesson to all team individuals; humans must check the manner to look at what they research in their day by day carrying sports, and organization-constructing meetings and events want to be scheduled regularly. This is the important shape of crew-constructing.

However, there are one of a kind alternatives that managers and educators can hire to talk greater correctly with their company individuals.

Some managers take delivery of as real with that including a competitive element to events, collectively with organization-constructing sports activities, is a practical technique to encourage employees each brief and long time.

If that is your intention, you could recollect dividing your group into or smaller companies and having them compete in brilliant sports activities activities sports and sports. This is pretty powerful at fostering group spirit and motivating employees to finish their assigned obligations.

The Important Role Of Strategy.

A manager or crew builder have to have a well-defined technique in thoughts earlier than organizing the occasion, at some degree within the occasion, and inside the aftermath. Effective group planning involves being privy to the meeting's motive and targets in advance.

Is there a problem with way standard overall performance or with inspiring personnel to carry out properly?

Is there new facts that need to be disclosed, or is it greater vital to increase recollect?

All of this should be assessed earlier than the assembly and guarded in institution-constructing sports activities. You need to form institution sports and the group(s) itself in the maximum efficient way feasible to perform the purpose.

Also, communication is vital. You have to speak the identical goals for your personnel in a clean and prepared way that permits you to don't forget the assembly's critical elements notwithstanding the reality that they do no longer endure in thoughts everything spoken. Instructions on what each crew member need to do should be specific and allotted to all crew people to make sure no character is left in the darkish.

Understanding group-constructing includes getting to know your teammates on a personal and professional diploma. A crew builder is aware about that even reputedly insignificant information which embody organizing teams or allocating unique folks to certainly one of a kind people can be a prison duty or an asset. As a forestall end result, group developers want to get to understand their teammates in my opinion and be familiar with the foremost archetypes of industrial company personalities.

What Methods Can I Use to Motivate My Team?

This is a regularly asked question when I art work with managers. Motivation check is tremendous, with every business organisation faculty, journal, and mag focusing on it. Theories abound. Motivation, in my revel in, isn't always a few element that can be "informed" in humans. It isn't a functionality or a potential.

Motivation is an inner technique fueled with the resource of our inner values and beliefs - the ones things which can be most vital to us. When you recognize the ones values and ideals, you could then decide the manner to encourage your people.

One opportunity is to infuse your control fashion with motivating behaviors. Managers that excel at this aren't most effective splendid managers however moreover superb leaders.

What does this suggest? Here are some sincere questions to ponder.

Be a chairman your worker's believe and recognize - This may also additionally sound self-evident, but don't forget and appreciate take time to expand and can be misplaced right away. Your deeds advantage your keep in mind and understand. How dependable are you?

Do you preserve your ensures?

Do you keep away from making unreliable guarantees?

Are you a defender of your humans?

Are you a lone wolf or organization participant?

Do you renowned your crew's accomplishments?

Know your team - This refers for your familiarity along side your teammates.

What are their alternatives and dislikes?

What do they keep highly-priced?

Is there no price?

What latent talents may additionally additionally they non-public that you could recognize and expand?

The handiest managers I've labored with have diagnosed this.

They have an uncanny capability to apprehend what makes their human beings tick. They make the effort to get to understand them, whether over a coffee or after paintings on the pub. They observe their realize-a way to elicit the best popular overall performance from their humans at the identical time as moreover addressing their requirements.

Provide your team with interesting and worrying paintings. Intelligent and formidable people enjoy stimulating work and having a say in what or how subjects are finished.

How frequently do you carry your personnel along in choice-making?

How effective are you at delegating responsibilities?

Do you delegate or micromanage your art work?

Do you assign them obligations an high-quality manner to assignment them and resource in their studying?

Do you help them of their instructional endeavors?

Be candid collectively collectively together with your remarks - Employees crave input, even hard comments.

How regularly do you provide remarks (aside from at some point of performance critiques)?

Do you sanitize your messages?

Do you awareness on the person's limiting behaviors and praise them?

Are you a train to your personnel?

While imparting honest comments, specially even as there are overall performance troubles, may be tough, it is able to be a brilliant motivator at the same time as done successfully. A corollary to this is how regularly do you solicit input out of your employees?

Communicate, Communicate - Communication is one of the quality motivational gadget you have got were given, and that is mainly proper during instances of exchange. How properly do your employees get the big photo - the goals, the method? How nicely do they understand their location within it? How are you capable of help them in figuring out their match?

Don't count on that surely because of the fact you noted a few thing as quick as, the message turn out to be received. Individuals apprehend records through the "lens" in their values and beliefs. Utilize top notch channels of conversation and, as normally, take into account that deeds talk louder than terms.

Motivating behaviors on my own won't ensure a endorsed organisation, and organizational issues are every so often past a supervisor's manage. However, specializing in what you could control (and influencing what you cannot) may fit an extended way in the path of growing worker motivation, loyalty, and productivity.

Therefore, managers, how do you encourage your groups?! Distribute your information!

Involve Everyone in Team-building Activities.

Team-building sports are an critical issue of learning the manner to guide a hard and fast efficiently. However, they will be extra than that. I'm curious what number of managers understand that we spend extra time with co-human beings than with our husbands, higher halves, youngsters, buddies, and one-of-a-kind own family people.

We typically understand very little approximately our co-employees. Nonetheless, we must negotiate, take route from, collaborate with, and get together with them every day. Wow.

When most humans go through in thoughts powerful enterprise-constructing sports activities and the manner to govern a set, they achieve this from a manager's mind-set. As the supervisor, they have to furthermore see via the worker's eyes. Why?

Because the worker can be responsible for all the duties assigned thru way of the supervisor. An worker's behavior has the power to make or spoil a fixed.

They need to understand the price of any crew improvement exercising. Then they should enjoy they're able to use the commands discovered. They should consider that the mind that group-constructing sports have tested are truly well well worth converting their behavior for.

Effective organization-building sports activities and identifying a manner to control a set start with the manager determining whether or not or not they and people they oversee have the same angle.

The exceptional fulfillment will rise up at the same time as employees enjoy participated inside the way of improving subjects. The manager's vision, on the other hand, need to be formed and defined. Some inquiries need to be made.

Why are we collaborating in team-constructing sporting activities?

What may be top notch after they have completed their work?

Will we be able to offer guidelines in the course of the manner?

Are subjects going to enhance, or will they stay as they'll be?

And how are we going to keep subjects higher than they have been earlier than?

Responding to those questions is essential to the group's overall performance following the team-constructing sporting sports. Following an powerful consultation (or series of intervals), the supervisor must control cooperative humans.

Issues want to be minimized. Every employee have to experience more confident approximately reporting to paintings every day. (This is the factor at which you agree to smile.)

What do crew-building sports activities suggest to you as an employee?

Are they full-size?

Are they useful?
Are they useless?

Or do they make contributions to developing going to paintings every day a higher enjoy than it became formerly? That is crucial.

The place of work need to be an improvement above what it have become previously. That is the objective that every manager should try for. Selecting profitable sports activities of the manager's time faraway from the place of business is vital if the manager wishes to have a more cohesive group than earlier than the sports.

The numerous sort of group-constructing gadget available to managers permits the improvement of teamwork. The purpose is to enhance how human beings collaborate typically. At a minimum, the questions posed under ought to be addressed as part of the making plans approach for choosing crew-building activities.

There are large benefits to choosing activities that inspire collaboration. The first is advanced system regular common performance, however the most terrific isn't addressing normal performance problems monthly.

Team-building physical video games are crucial in any place of business putting, although the group participants are geographically dispersed. These sports help to break the ice amongst co-employees and provide managers with an possibility to get to understand their group members on a greater private level.

The office team of workers contributors come from wonderful backgrounds and because of this want to speak correctly. As a stop end result, the arrival of group bonding ideas is crucial to break the ice.

The manager's process and responsibility are to embody every person in team bonding activities. Here are a few simple strategies for sporting out this with out causing an excessive amount of disruption:

Include amusement: Any group-constructing sports sports that do not prevent with the group smiling and growing extremely good reminiscences. A aggregate of 70% enjoyment and 30% artwork guarantees the interest's fulfillment. Also, avoid excessively emphasizing the a laugh; as an alternative, allow everyone to be themselves and have a examine crew bonding thoughts as enjoyable.

Your corporation includes the following human beings: Recognize the group's profile. In this manner, you will be privy to their benefits and drawbacks. Attempt to test their personal histories and lifestyles. This will assist you in identifying the regions of the business enterprise that require hobby.

Contact: Team bonding techniques that don't entail a excessive diploma of touch and interplay a number of the human beings are ineffective. To ensure the exercise's effectiveness, it is crucial to provide human beings with a shared platform for verbal exchange. Divide the team members into businesses composed of a very good blend of human beings with various functions.

We stated that the activities need to be a laugh, however you need to constantly maintain the 30% tough art work element.

67

They turns into bored inside the event that they cannot join the hobby to three component in their art work environment.

This allows kids apprehend the cost of teamwork. You can be a part of the sports activities to video video games and other sports through citing some thing alongside the strains of, "This is similar to when the Xyz crew finished the subsequent hobby and."

The length of activities is important to take into account. It is generally final to spread duties in some unspecified time in the future of the hour rather than having a unmarried hobby drag on for hours. Evenly spaced sports activities decorate your interest span and help keep the 'amusing' component.

Always have backup and trade sports activities available if one interest fails to interact individuals otherwise you can't keep organization individuals' interest.

Team-Building Events And Expectations.

Another trap-all word that we as managers regularly listen and try to reply to is "crew-constructing." Team-building isn't always a fad. Too regularly, but, a set-constructing event is selected, planned, and executed with out regard for the institution-building exercise. A group improvement exercising or occasion will no longer treatment or even address the subsequent:

Low Morale - Using a set-constructing exercise to combat low morale does not artwork or resolve the underlying hassle. Low worker morale is a symptom of a larger hassle in the branch, employer, or commercial enterprise enterprise. Taking a day off to speak or undertake organisation activities to unite the institution will no longer resolve the underlying trouble.

Tool for Change Management - A group-constructing workout isn't a tool for change control. While in contemporary years, as budgets are being squeezed to a breaking thing, many leaders were inclined to conflate the two. It is important that we, as leaders, offer the ones very top notch duties the eye they want.

Communication development - Like low morale, verbal exchange is an internal trouble that can't be resolved with a yearly shot of group-constructing.

Team-constructing events aren't the time or area to deliver terrible statistics approximately the enterprise or enterprise company. Too often, I've witnessed those physical sports devolve into a few humans defensive a big organization captive, forcing others to rehash every unpleasant trouble of the paintings environment.

What is a Team-building Event's Purpose?

The intention of a set-building event is to show your personnel to possibilities to increase new competencies or explore novel thoughts and procedures to common troubles in a non-threatening environment.

The software program isn't supposed to function an extended training session for body of workers people who already very own or are currently gaining new talents on the task. Nor is it the intention to teach frame of human beings and employees on what they "want to" be doing to carry out their jobs extra effectively.

Other than that, the event must offer first-rate and upsetting alternatives to fashionable behaviors. It must encourage your employees to attempt new matters, expect in any other case, and step outside the "subject" to look in the event that they personal a capability set they have never considered applying of their present day feature interior your employer.

Conducting an Assessment of Your Team-building Activities and Expectations.

Unfortunately, group development sports are often thrown collectively in a 2d of desperation. We lease people no longer affiliated with our enterprise, product, or issuer to facilitate sports, plan activities, and so on, "hoping" that the facilitators ought to deliver what the personnel dreams.

Before choosing a fixed-building workout, it's miles important which you, due to the fact the leader, have a test the want for the hobby and your expectancies for the hobby. First, you want to define what a Team-constructing Activity is and the expectancies you have got got for the hobby.

I've witnessed some outstanding group-constructing sports and had been commemorated to talk at a few. Therefore, I'd want to spend some time highlighting a number of the elements that contributed to those group-building sports being so memorable, well-attended, and properly-obtained thru employees, leaders, and site visitors.

Planning.

A group-building occasion requires the same degree of training and planning as a convention or incredible profits occasion. This occasion want to be more than an afternoon spent paying attention to or collaborating within the leader's favored hobby or, worse, being attentive to a speaker uncommon with the challenge and has not carried out their homework.

When arranging the event, primarily based, planned seminars tailored on your group's specific goals need to be blanketed. This will depend on the size of your business enterprise. The event's enterprise should be similar to that of a properly-run conference or workshop. Dates and signal-up office work ought to comprise all personnel humans and a gap for remarks.

The agenda may additionally want to look a few issue like this:

In 40-5 mins, we will begin with a welcome and evaluation of the day's sports, observed via using introductions of the workshop leaders and facilitators, the places of huge centers, and a speak of non-compulsory activities. Please endure in mind that non-obligatory sports are that; there want to in no way be any pressure to participate in optionally available sports activities.

15-minute intermission.

45 to 60 minutes Workshops I and II.

Workshop I - Inspirational and upbeat - The problem might be dealing with tough people to verbal exchange techniques. Still, the important thing terms proper right here are uplifting and inspirational.

How many workshops have you ever attended in which the hassle seemed very relevant primarily based totally on the discover however rapid found out itself to be a dreary presentation of some "no longer so exciting" slides that did not solution any questions or excite you inside the slightest?

Workshop II - An hour of skills improvement with a twist.

How frequently have you ever ever questioned, as an individual, "How did they try this?" "Man, I preference I knew extra approximately that." We do now not have time to "research" non-traditional talents at some point of our worrying workdays.

This is an exquisite possibility to provide your humans and employees the opportunity to analyze and take a look at a skills set in which they'll excel. This is also excessive first-class for you as a pacesetter, as you're boosting your in-house abilities pool.

These guides are held concurrently; via signing up for one or the alternative, people decide to gaining knowledge of some issue new and being surely recommended to carry their new capabilities and information lower returned to their workplace. Each session want to encompass at the very least seminars to permit your employees to make growth-improving selections.

Lunch - 60 mins - is a time for networking. Tables need to be set up in order that various corporations, now not "buddies," sit down down together, and every table need to have at the least one chief or supervisor (in listening mode). It's awesome how open human beings turn out to be when they percentage lunch with strangers, even when a leader or boss is there.

45 to 60 minutes Workshops III and IV.

- Workshops III and IV are dependent similarly to the previous workshops. Although the priority count is unique, it despite the truth that includes relevant records that staff will like being attentive to approximately.

Closing - The stop want to be inspirational and ceremonial. Employees who have contributed immensely to the corporation's achievement should be commemorated right here. This is the time a great way to deliver an motive behind for your employees why they're precious assets and make a contribution to their achievement.

As you can see from the itinerary above, a well designed group-constructing occasion can will let you spend a very effective day and drastically improve your commercial enterprise growth.

When taken into consideration as an afterthought, the occasion does not carry out as properly. Preparation is critical to the success of any opportunity you create as a pacesetter, whether or not to your personnel or your purchaser base.

Cost.

The fee of a set-building event can range from less expensive to prohibitively steeply-priced. Here are a few examples of organization-building sports that I surely have facilitated or been a part of. The picnic region of a public park come to be used, and the concurrent workshops had been held below park timber.

Due to the low rate of the grounds, my associate employed a fish fry corporation to cater the event; a realtor friend rented a large empty residence to some other associate; another time, because of the low price of the day's rental (rental of tables, furniture, and so on.), the catering changed into incredible;

A close by museum in our region has brilliant, unused meeting rooms. Again, a small charge consequences in a giant impact.

Whether you are operating on a shoestring charge range or not, it's far critical to keep in mind that your employees are clients really as an lousy lot because the customers for whom you conduct workshops, seminars, and conferences.

Finally, the price is small, and the underlying motive of the team-constructing event is progressed via advanced impact and employee dedication to destiny desires.

Increase Competitiveness Through Team-Building Activities.

Competitiveness is essential to every enterprise's success in ultra-modern globalized surroundings. Today's extremely dynamic global market necessitates competitiveness in products and services and, maximum crucially, groups. Most corporations location a top class on corporation cohesiveness and engagement even as keeping a competitive spirit at the sidelines.

Team competitiveness is depending on motivation, region, and proper help. However, it may be the figuring out aspect between your crew's effectiveness and the rest of the corporate vicinity. Team-building research and sports offer an wonderful opportunity to foster that spirit.

Four strategies for growing competition at some point of institution-building sports activities embody the subsequent:

1. Establish the tone.

Before challenge a crew-building hobby, set up the tone. While most individuals recognize sports as natural amusement, they apprehend that competitiveness plays a tremendous function in crew-constructing. Selecting a selected definition will help participants in becoming higher aligned with the commercial enterprise agency's purpose, imaginative and prescient, and values.

2. Be the primary to take the initiative.

Encourage every group to take the initiative at some point of each team-building workout. You can also award teams that take the initiative; human beings with a killer spirit usually take the initiative in any assignment, artwork or challenge.

Once taking component agencies are forced to take the initiative, they may obviously increase their bravery. Many institution-constructing bodily video games are performed with the useful resource of decent establishments that design sports that encourage initiative.

3. Establish expectancies.

To assemble a competitive mind-set, it's far maximum famous to set up smooth expectations. Establishing crystal clear opportunities lets in businesses to awareness and concentrate their efforts.

Setting expectancies is likewise a important element of effective teamwork. This will increase the productiveness and competitiveness of your team. This moreover improves reason consistency and promotes inexperienced use of critical sources like people, time, and coins.

four. Teach steam people a manner to resolve conflicts.

Excessive opposition should probable increase conflict. It is your sole responsibility to train them at the first rate strategies for resolving internal and outside disputes. This is critical within the competitive mentality. Through institution-building wearing activities, you could teach your crew to be well mannered and manipulate opinions. Place them in an environment that exams their group spirit.

It is truely beneficial to prepare an off-website group-building hobby that lets in personnel to interact and bond. Trekking can be an exceptional organization-constructing activity. Allow personnel to get together and face a project as a group toward the backdrop of appropriate locations.

The four techniques referred to above will boom your personnel' competitiveness and help your business enterprise expand at a price in no way seen in advance than.

The Fundamentals Of Diversity Management In Team Building.

At its middle, variety manipulate promotes collaboration amongst employees. Its assignment is to bring ladies and men from numerous backgrounds together and mildew them into an effective group targeted on a not unusual reason.

This allows large-scale responsibilities to be completed efficiently and with few headaches. Typically, undertaking managers might lead this shape of education with team-constructing thoughts, guiding personnel through one in every of a kind team-building bodily sports.

Individuals should first find out how to talk with each exclusive. One approach is to divide a huge company of humans into subgroups and ask each member to take a look at the backgrounds and personalities of the others. This permits crew members to emerge as extra acquainted with each other and better recognize what human beings have encountered of their private lives.

Also, personnel can be required to wait a series of training courses wherein preconceptions are deconstructed and debunked. These preconceptions may be primarily based on a person's coloration, sexual orientation, or age. Often, a psychologist or sociology expert can be invited in to provide advice and spark communique. Employees are frequently suggested to take part actively.

Also, organisation dynamics sports can be blanketed within the consultation. This can variety from doing surveys to replying to inquiries with a raised hand in the air. This can provide notion into humans's preferred attitudes closer to unique topics and beneficial aid in developing an regular agreement on some essential problems.

Managers need to set up without a doubt described desires and educate all team individuals that non-public critiques may be completed based totally mostly on those goals. When fulfillment is defined, group participants apprehend what they want to do to carry out efficiently and earn promotions. They should be all proper shifting earlier if they comply with instructions and obtain assigned work.

Occasionally, it's far useful for institution contributors to accumulate outdoor of the workplace in a low-key region. Whether at a bowling alley, a restaurant, or a wearing event, this may assist foster camaraderie and introduce others to one another.

This is specially important on the subject of bringing together employees who couldn't in any other case engage. Once ladies and men higher apprehend every one-of-a-kind's strengths, all additives of the assignment ought to characteristic extra without problems.

In any occasion, challenge managers ought to ensure that sports are short and to the factor. This ought to expand a experience of network amongst all the ones involved. Also, it have to allow them time to do their normal artwork responsibilities and other chores on time desk.

When brainstorming institution-constructing mind, managers should recollect sports activities that convey collectively humans of diverse ethnicities, sexual orientations, a long term, religions, and creeds.

By supporting men and women in seeing the good in others, those personnel will greater with out problems be conscious their co-humans' abilties and understanding, which can be applied to their time-commemorated success.

Chapter 5: Open Lines Of Communication To Engage Everyone.

The purpose of group-building activities and conferences is to get sincerely every body in a agency or branch to artwork cooperatively towards a common motive. Communication is an vital element of this. Whether via e mail, cellphone, or in man or woman, masses of encounters arise every day in every place of job, retail, and warehouse.

Team-constructing sports activities attempt to instill the essential importance of open verbal exchange amongst all enterprise participants. Any communique breakdown might also have immoderate outcomes. There are many reasons for a verbal exchange breakdown, but 3 of the maximum preferred are indexed right here.

1. The effect of the silo.

While it may seem self-obvious that withholding facts can create issues, communique breakdowns are not generally deliberate. If a collection member is uncomfortable interacting with their teammates or believes their enter is unimportant, withholding statistics should in all likelihood prevent the rest of the crew from functioning, and they could.

This is probably because of competitiveness, geographical separation, or separate groups that do not need to percent with each specific corporation. This has been proven frequently on the institution improvement lessons I facilitate.

There are many motives for the silo effect. Still, it's far tough for the organisation to feature at top common overall performance and effectiveness with out tearing down partitions and fostering collaboration among all teams. Once the agencies recognize they want to artwork together to cope with the problems, the "team-constructing" portion of the interest is complete.

2. Each person is huge.

A common impediment to conversation is a reluctance to talk candidly with senior manipulate. Participating in organisation-building sports activities sports requiring each person to art work collaboratively to clear up riddles or puzzles demonstrates that everyone is an imperative group member.

I recall one event wherein the teams and judges protected every body worried inside the mission. From the meeting line employees to the engineers and bosses, every person come to be at the same organization.

It changed into eye-beginning to take a look at how unique degrees handled problem-solving. When a hard and fast recognizes the importance that each member gives, they might form bonds. When immoderate manage recognizes that their agency's fulfillment is contingent on every person from manage on down, it can effect its morale.

three. Fear of being incorrect.

Some personnel may be hesitant to offer critiques that I reflect adversely on them. While no longer each concept is a exceptional one, personnel can take a look at although they do no longer see an immediate effect on their contribution.

Managers can examine the concerns or hurdles that employees enjoy and the reasons for those troubles. Any enter demonstrates to a commercial organization what its employees are questioning and what they charge. Being capable of listen to an worker without passing judgment allows installation receive as actual with.

Understanding and addressing the issues that employees confront and keeping open lines of communication move a protracted way inside the route of focusing anybody on the institution's or organization's shared purpose.

While communication on my own can not assure corporation success, a lack of it significantly will growth failure. Team-constructing sports are an high-quality technique to hold the crew collectively and change the present day setting.

Successful Team-constructing Techniques for Managers.

Your crew is your agency's spine. How nicely the whole thing functions together and the way you lead it could make or destroy your business enterprise's achievement. Team-constructing may be tough. Each group member gives a totally particular set of capabilities and weaknesses to the table.

As the manager and team leader, you furthermore mght have skills and shortcomings that make a contribution to your crew's success. In cutting-edge aggressive corporation, knowledge the manner to link the puzzle quantities of a a achievement organization is crucial. Here are few tips to help you in forming a a fulfillment institution.

Understand How You Work.

To begin, you want to apprehend the manner you characteristic.

How may you describe your control style?

Are you an exceptional communicator and an effective chief?

Conduct an vital appraisal of your self, genuinely as you may an employee, and stay receptive to regions for increase. Perhaps you want to decorate your verbal exchange abilities or learn how to lead through example. Perhaps earnings or management schooling may want to benefit your manipulate style and assist you in growing a a success group.

Recognize Your Team.

Your team people are more than most effective a set of our our bodies stuffed into desk seats. They are humans with diverse personalities, and every contributes a completely unique factor of the business enterprise to the organization. Make an effort to get to recognize your teammates. Each week, time desk time for the agency to gather, lighten up and get to understand each different.

This revel in of camaraderie strengthens relationships among crew participants and permits the crew to function extra successfully as an entire. Also, if each institution member feels tremendous and respected, your group might be more powerful because everybody feels preferred and recognizes their mind and skills.

Roles and Responsibilities Are Clearly Defined.

Once you have got gotten to understand each team member and identified their strengths and boundaries, you may outline each group member's obligations and duties. Perhaps one team member isn't always particularly professional at their profession however excels at maintaining the group heading within the right course.

This individual will make a contribution appreciably to the crew's fulfillment via the usage of preserving the organization moving and saving you money by means of preserving off terrible judgments or allowing the institution to stagnate.

Another group member may additionally additionally non-public first rate communication skills and the ability to relate to a sizable shape of human beings. This person is treasured because of the truth they could define the organization's desires and effectively speak them to its members.

Your organization is just like a puzzle made from many precise components. You have to understand how they all healthy together and the jobs they every perform on the squad. You also can additionally then capitalize on their strengths and talents and genuinely define their roles in the group to make sure that it capabilities properly.

Recognize that remarks is a -manner avenue.

Feedback is a priceless useful aid. It informs you of your crew's overall performance and places for development. You can have a right or informal remarks gadget. By being proactive with remarks, you may assist your body of workers in enhancing each day and heading off excessive problems. Avoid being a reactive manager; as an alternative, be proactive via taking note of your team's input and providing effective feedback of your private.

Recognize, Respect, and Commend.

Everybody enjoys being rewarded, and each person values appreciate. Recognize and recognize a team member who is going above and past. This demonstrates your corporation's sincerely certainly well worth, and they will exert extended attempt closer to their aim. Take time to revel in your accomplishments.

Even minor accomplishments deserve popularity, whilst easy as having field lunches furnished within the future. Positive reinforcement and recognition will help in motivating and keeping your institution's determination to walking nicely together.

As a set leader and manager, you are responsible for developing an effective team and maintaining them heading within the right route. Utilize those 5 strategies to form a a fulfillment team and whole the undertaking at hand.

When you apprehend your group's strengths and obstacles, you may collaborate to set up an powerful and a hit institution so one can't high-quality meet however surpass your business corporation's dreams.

Improve The Effectiveness Of Your Team-Building Strategy.

Yes, it's miles critical to paintings in your team dynamics each day, tracking and enhancing as vital. However, particularly advanced business enterprise-constructing days have their region. Just keep in mind that in case you're going to host a group-building event, it want to provide charge. After all, schooling is pricey, or even individuals anticipate a move lower back on their time and effort.

It is beside the thing when you have interplay in group-constructing sports, collect a listing of team tips or communicate group issues. What topics most is the manner you perform a little aspect, now not what you do. Understanding what companies require to function well will will will let you recognize higher the way to enhance organization procedures (no longer surely in the path of a specific team-building event however furthermore on a day by day basis).

What Teams Require.

To be effective - to characteristic as a cohesive unit and attain extra than is viable in my view - corporations require a few crucial components of their environment. While attaining the ones developments isn't always hard, they do need some art work at the element of the crew chief or organization proprietor.

These elements were proven over and over in research to be vital for effective businesses. They aren't "new age," "touchy-feely," or "time-wasters." They are the fundamentals of teamwork, and corporations that recognize their charge and are looking for to maintain them are rewarded with teams that outperform their extra normal opposite numbers with the aid of way of a massive margin.

Strengthening Team Performance.

If you intend to boost your crew's overall performance, it's far now not first-class approximately "whipping them into form." It's about installing location the superior setting for them to carry out at their peak.

It's additionally approximately accepting and expertise your mission as a leader/train and growing the capabilities crucial to assemble the team you deserve. As the arena's greatest carrying coaches often u . S . A ., the teach's profession is jeopardized even as a group fails to carry out!

Therefore, allow us to have a have a have a look at what a set calls for to be effective.

The Five Areas of Effectiveness.

1. Mission of the Team. Every member of the group need to understand why the organization plays what it does. What is the business trying to carry out, and the way does the crew contribute to this try?

Every group member need to understand the group's priorities, particularly once they trade and the way operating to the wrong priorities impairs the institution's ability to execute its motive.

2. Goal Accomplishment. The crew leader's function is to assist the institution in defining their desires (each collective and person) and provide feedback on their development in the route of accomplishing the ones desires. This need to be steady, truthful, and non-blaming.

The group, every collectively and for my part, have to moreover make contributions to the improvement of these objectives. Above all, the institution chief have to assist the team in reaching its goals via providing help and belongings.

three. Self-willpower. While the institution must paintings in the route of attaining corporation desires and in keeping with enterprise organisation norms, the institution and its humans require a few degree of autonomy in desire-making and hobby.

That doesn't imply a few aspect is going. Still, it does suggest that we all have a voice in our every day lives, which incorporates our professional existence, in location of enforcing authority; try to amplify a set's skills diploma via steering.

Both technical and interpersonal abilities (together called Emotional Intelligence) are necessary for crew people to count on possession in their jobs and act appropriately.

Guidance and position modeling will foster possession and independence, permitting the crew leader to "delegate" many operational chores and consciousness on extra vital manage duties.

4. Transparent, forthright communication. Communication should be candid, properly timed, and -way. This is not a maintain near-slave relationship but as an alternative an engagement among adults on an same footing (of course, this takes a excessive level

of emotional intelligence from both occasions).

When personnel are treated with dignity and recognize, the huge majority respond with elevated try to outcomes. When every body feels comfortable civilly expressing themselves, the entire crew plays higher and the consumer notices! Conflict is minimized and addressed extra brief, and people have a better control on their behaviors.

five. Positive feature fashions and social requirements. Individuals observe exceptional through statement, evaluation, and exercising.

What are they watching in your commercial company when they examine the Team Leader's conduct?

Are the Team Leader and all one-of-a-kind supervisors demonstrating the shape of conduct they want their team individuals to show off?

Or is it greater of a "do as I say, no longer as I do" scenario?

Team individuals should have incredible characteristic fashions, and time and effort want to be invested in schooling and capabilities development to extract the maximum fashionable usual overall performance from each team member.

Finally, crew-constructing is a vital thing of your complete business organization improvement plan. Do not use it as a band-useful resource or a panacea; it's miles useless in each cases. It have to float in reality from the severa regular movements you perform to keep your team healthy.

Using Team-constructing Games to Rethink Group Strategy.

Focusing on group techniques and emphasizing severa strengths and shortcomings via crew-constructing sports activities can extensively growth any agency or corporation's productivity.

Using critical mental concepts and set up values, devoted alternate control teachers also can assist any team in achieving extra achievement of their paintings surroundings.

Stimulating and exciting sports sports indoors or exterior in exceptional locations at some stage in the united states of the united states can be an awesome method for any enterprise enterprise to set new priorities and adaptable strategies.

Teammates can benefit a modern mind-set at the administrative center and gain from new techniques and wondering. Utilizing a totally jail group-constructing path may want to make all of the distinction in presenting a required decorate to a organization group.

The Positive Consequences of Problem Solving.

Each employer and worker confronts everyday limitations and troubles that must be addressed and resolved. The gap amongst a success and failed groups is frequently determined through their ability to clear up those problems.

This is without a doubt one area in which organization institution-building video video video games can be beneficial. Group strengthening sports can assist boom morale and decorate communication for human beings and institution members primarily based on important mental requirements.

Fully popular institution improvement teachers may also foster group development in any other case via removing individuals from their everyday art work contexts to cognizance on important skills. A working break at one of the u . S . A .'s many locales would possibly display to be a vast and profitable funding for any commercial enterprise company or agency.

How Team-constructing Games Can Help You Feel More Satisfied With Your Job.

Every supervisor and crew chief ought to be involved with growing worker and colleague interest pleasure and morale. Many studies have decisively tested that contented personnel are greater powerful and in the end extra useful to their employers than disgruntled employees.

Therefore, it must be the purpose of each prudent manager to hire any method that improves these important perceptions of cost and well nicely worth. A absolutely accepted organization technique route is one of the exceptional strategies to perform this.

Qualified instructors can collaborate with team leaders and bosses to create a application tailored to each group of work-mates and co-humans' precise desires. Indoor and outside team-constructing sports activities activities might also want to make a sizeable difference in phrases of improving place of job relationships and communication.

Businesses and companies of a wide variety can appreciably benefit from such artwork breaks and is probably well to research the ability advantages.

Team-constructing Facilitation and Mentoring.

Do mentors play a function in crew improvement? They seem to achieve this, and it moreover stands to cause that once a strong team member mentors a newcomer or a weaker organization member, the effects are remarkable. It's thrilling to peer what that more younger or greater moderen group member is able to conducting.

As a supervisor, it's far crucial to facilitate this form of mentorship among pick out business enterprise people while dealing with them. If the institution has 3 or four strong gamers, each of them must friend one or of the squad's junior individuals. Attempting to installation commonplace bonds will help on this approach.

There are severa techniques to carry out this, and with the proper facilitation, it could grow to be as natural as riding a bicycle. All too often, junior group people are aware that they can not compete on the identical degree as senior group people who very own the vital credentials and experience to play.

However, this doesn't advocate that they may now not achieve this inside the destiny; it is crucial to pair them with a superstar with the right mentality to make sure their success.

Not each extremely good player possesses the persona attributes or the staying strength to characteristic a father discern to individuals of the junior squad. Many lack the potential, and they will be able to do extra harm than precise to a younger crew member.

When dealing with a group, it's miles critical to perceive which personnel can assist others and convey the rest of the organization up. Nonetheless, some person sorts are capable of filling this hobby. I desire you could recall this.

Promotion is constantly a substantial event. The most difficult factor is continuously stepping up and not hiding in the back of what you used to accomplish at your preceding art work. The transition from Manager to Executive is one of the maximum large.

Executives should hold in thoughts and act on troubles that are pretty first-rate from the ones faced thru their manipulate contrary numbers. The first-class way to summarize is that we should expect and manage strategically, which isn't always a few issue that most people are familiar with.

There is some different difficulty as well. Executive corporations are normally made from in addition induced and pushed human beings. Any institution with too many similarities and no longer enough variances risks turning into unbalanced to the point of sickness and falling victim to "groupthink," wherein group contributors agree on the entirety, even if their selections are extensively incorrect. Executive crew-constructing may be useful.

Undoubtedly, one of the commonalities can be that each one group individuals can be smart sufficient to conquer the team's weaknesses in the event that they draw close them within the first area. Thus, if a nicely-selected institution pastime assists them in identifying the problem, the group can begin to mend itself.

To summarize, if an executive team chooses a collection-constructing desire, it should reputation on strategic manipulate. During the fast, it will find out crew shortcomings and provoke putting in vicinity measures to avoid them.

When it involves walking strategically, the primary problem that any new Executive has is defining a way. Not what "their" plan is however how one appears in exercising. A technique is a hybrid of a imaginative and prescient, a purpose, and a way. It is the holiday spot an agency desires to attain, the timeframe it wants to be there, and the technique it desires to examine along the way.

Strategic management is ready imposing the plan continually in some unspecified time in the future of the organization to make it useful and in the long run powerful. Each employee should understand what it approach for his or her hobby and use it whilst making everyday decisions, and strategic manage is all approximately bringing that vision to fruition.

Generally, crew-building sports are not designed to draw interest to strategic issues. Tactical selection-making is generally the order of the day. Those adept at "taking photos from the hip" fare higher than folks who determine upon to devise meticulously in advance than starting.

Thus, the activity chosen must undergo this in thoughts. The exercising need to be whole and prolonged sufficient to provide strategic thinkers a proper threat to steer the institution's technique. It must furthermore allow agencies to hire that technique sooner or later of the pastime so that the success or failure of the employer's method can be evaluated during debriefing.

When it entails debriefing, that consultation is the most critical component of the whole workout. The approach need to be well idea out and extensively talking conducted by manner of the team itself to sincerely select out the group's flaws. That is, it have to be documented.

A facilitator's feature at this component need to be to help the team in figuring out the disturbing situations created with the useful resource of way in their method to the task, no longer to stand inside the the the front and tell them wherein they went wrong. That no longer regularly assists a collection in comprehending the to be had learning or moving it to the administrative center, wherein it could make a difference.

When making plans a collection away day for government-degree managers, don't forget which you have to provide them a few factor suitable for his or her shape of crew and venture. That is an first-rate method!

Chapter 6: Building An Effective Team

You've heard me say in distinctive Concise Reads courses that no person is born one manner or any other and I argue for nurture vs. Nature or the belief that conduct, mind, even personalities may be taught and untaught rather than believing that we are born with a specific predilection and that can't be changed. I say this because of the truth this is precisely what occurs in BUILDING an powerful team. Notice that I didn't say PICKING an effective organization. The resume only tells you within the event that they're certified for a method. There's however art work to be finished to assemble an effective group.

Team Building Framework:

If we pick out human beings we've worked nicely within the beyond, we but want to assemble the crew. So how are we able to BUILD a crew regardless of who the employer individuals are? It's clean and I've executed it commonly within the past. What we need to bear in mind is a easy framework called the E3 or E-cubed group framework which incorporates Endorsement, Execution, and Excitement.

Endorsement: The group have to be aligned in its cause and its ideals. Before starting the challenge, the manager want to recognize if each organization member can without problems endorse the undertaking. If they can not gather this with out issue, then the supervisor should push to find out the idea reasons. If the team members (doesn't need to be all, although it's really one member) cannot without troubles endorse the project, then the manager want to draft a file of guiding ideas that participants want to agree upon. These guiding thoughts are a proxy for endorsement of the assignment itself.

For instance, allow's say that a large business enterprise is planning a trade in which they have got agreed to lessen five% of brand new walking fees with the aid of the following 6 months. Some group individuals ought to probably suppose it is not feasible to perform, or that cutting fees is inside the direction of their morale nature if it manner that someone down the street this shape of client or worker could be affected. Whatever the case can be, they without a doubt do no longer feel comfortable to recommend a price reducing diploma. That's accurate enough to voice via the way, because we need actual endorsement on the way to advantage fulfillment. In this situation, we might draft a fixed of guiding requirements that the organization can agree on. This set of guiding ideas will possibly encompass the subsequent:

• We will strive to ensure the corporation is in proper monetary health

• We will make an effort to put off as an entire lot as 5% of waste

• We will art work together to find synergistic relationships actually so our colleagues do not do the equal artwork or must do it twice because of negative conversation

As you may see, those guiding standards allow for higher purchase-in, alignment, or endorsement in preference to an poor fee-lowering undertaking.

You need to benefit endorsement.

I've visible the results of not attaining endorsement early on commonly earlier than. Members are assigned to a crew but best commit 50% of their energy to execution due to the reality they do no longer virtually suggest the task of the crew challenge.

Execution: This is the second problem of constructing an powerful organization and it includes the crucial equipment of feedback and education. We touched gently on comments and will communicate extra about it within the subsequent section. In addition to remarks and schooling, an effective group calls for clean roles and strategies. Processes need to be built for:

1. Communication

2. Conflict choice, and

3. Project control monitoring.

These three strategies have to be agreed upon inside the endorsement segment and then require periodic test-ins to regulate. In our 'Problem Solving' Concise Reads guide we learn how to deconstruct a hassle into its additives and assign proprietors to each issue. The way of monitoring requires assigned owners and tracking of outputs. Make positive the monitoring tool is publically viewable in order that each member isn't simplest accountable to you however to the crew as properly due to the fact that is a crew attempt.

As a supervisor and chief you may quick apprehend that you don't want to check in as often as you think you need to as soon as procedures are in place for communique, war selection, and project manage tracking.

In the 1990s I would possibly have recommended remarkable spreadsheets and tables that have helped me put together and become aware about the ones techniques for effective execution. However, these days it makes no feel to teach you antiquated equipment. Instead, I'll assist you to discover common PM device along aspect asana, wrike, trello, basecamp, or jira.

Many of these virtual equipment are built on the KANBAN technique) Which makes use of a Kanban board. Kanban grow to be a visualization at the begin advanced as a part of Toyota's lean production--lean in the revel in that it is supposed to cast off waste from multitasking and interruptions. The Kanban board indicates the paintings in improvement for each organization member, and lets in participants to pull a workstream this is ready or pending in region of the supervisor pushing responsibilities onto the institution member. Once this is finished the member takes ownership of the assignment and tally of finished tasks is shown. If a member goals assist to finish a project, this can also be visualized at the Kanban board.

Excitement: It's been the traditional modus operandi (M.O for quick) of enterprise managers to govern TIME. That in no way labored and first-rate reduced the quantity of fulfillment an employee obtained from his or her employment.

In truth, if you examine excessive churn groups in which personnel depart after one or extra years, you may find out that the managers there predominantly manipulate time.

The supervisor may check each hour or with the aid of way of e-mail, at once message, smartphone name, or in person. Slack has been used greater in recent times due to this, however while the tool may be used for proper with the useful resource of permitting organization individuals a platform for short conversation, it can also be used for evil whilst managers ping continually and the worker starts offevolved to construct tension that they might have unnoticed a message from their supervisor simply so they click on on-take a look at constantly in the end of the day.

Some managers will say they have got to check in as regularly as they do due to the fact employees are lazy. Well laziness mixed with strain will offer you with an ever poorer tremendous of labor. Sure, the artwork may be accomplished but it will in all likelihood be of terrible first-class, and you run the hazard of getting the employee leave the agency and having to retrain some different worker.

I've additionally had exceptional managers inform me, 'Well, I only need personnel who want to be proper right here, properly riddance to folks who left'. That again is a fault of the manager who exceptional manages time. The personnel who stayed absolutely wanted the paycheck, otherwise they too would have left.

Purposely having compelled it sufficient, I take delivery of as proper with, that element manipulate is the worst shape of control. I want you to now embody, recommend, and take transport of as proper with in ENERGY manipulate.

As a supervisor you need to have a pulse test for your organization's energy. Are they fulfilled? Are they effective? Do they revel in conflicted? Is there struggle amongst them? Do they need outside facts? By feeling the power of the crew, you will be capable of adapt and alternate the team dynamics to continuously enhance strength degrees in an effort to maximize productiveness. A easy instance that happened truly closing week modified into while a member of the institution who was liable for the format of our advertising and advertising advertising and marketing marketing campaign felt their mind did no longer make it to the preliminary draft and they were lots much less than excited to 'suppose out of doors the field' or to be innovative. I positioned that when I asked 'Hey Julia, why don't you provide you with the colors you believe you studied could paintings in this example. I accept as authentic collectively along with your expertise'. And Julia responded with 'Oh it is ideal enough. If the team we should me apprehend what colorings they want, I'll definitely consist of those within the layout'. That's all it took for me to recognise we needed to pause and refresh. So I requested the design team to go through a 48 hour sprint and begin the ideation method from scratch and note in the event that they however align at the contemporary-day layout we've set forth.

The very last marketing advertising campaign became a amazing fulfillment, and the most critical remarks from customers have become how a lot they preferred the design!

Managing pleasure is as a substitute crucial for building an effective institution, mainly if the assignment is going to take numerous weeks or months. Always have a finger at the strength pulse and your group will thank you for it and your boss will thank you even greater.

Managing strength in place of time have become highlighted in a Harvard Business Review article on a control initiative at Wachovia that noticed up to 20% boom in productiveness through ensuring power changed into optimized thru education. This is an excerpt at the test layout

"In early 2006 we took 106 personnel at 12 local banks in southern New Jersey via a curriculum of four modules, every of which centered on precise strategies for strengthening one of the 4 crucial dimensions of electricity. We added it at one-month intervals to agencies of approximately 20 to 25, starting from senior leaders to lower-level managers. We also assigned each attendee a fellow employee as a deliver of assist among instructions. Using Wachovia's private key preferred normal overall performance metrics, we evaluated how the participant agency accomplished in assessment with a group of employees at similar ranges at a close-by set of Wachovia banks who did now not go through the training. To create a reputable basis for evaluation, we looked at three hundred and sixty five days-over-one year percentage adjustments in performance throughout severa metrics."

Many Fortune 100 groups have instructional modules made to be had for their employees. Even the American Medical Association calls for hospitals to educate their medical medical doctors what accurate sleep hygiene looks as if.

This is want to be a stylish service everywhere (hint on your next startup). This Concise Reads wishes you as a future manager and leader to take the combat to the frontline in the place of work.

Team Building Productivity Cycle:

Now that we've located the three Es of building an effective organization, allow's now test a the productivity cycle that is massive in these days's most inexperienced businesses (sooner or later the naming).

Productivity Cycle: This is based mostly on responsibility and putting a cadence for the corporation. Accountability is crucial for personnel to take ownership of the output and remaining dates. Cadence is crucial as it has been verified that once groups comply with a every day or weekly regular, they begin to order the manner they paintings so there are fewer delays, interruptions, and idle time. This is extra right for businesses that require greater collaboration than character artwork.

The productiveness cycle commonly consists of regular meetings, manager aid, and common performance metrics :

1. Daily stand up conferences or huddles, weekly barometers, and weekly or month-to-month all-hands intervals: Whether daily and/or weekly, there can be a coming together of all individuals of a crew for an update on what development each member has made. This may be physical or virtual, however there wishes to be a feel that an 'update' is due. This gadgets the internal clock of a set. Huddles and stand-up conferences are thru way of definition very short, assume--15 minutes on common. This is virtually to get a pulse at the team device. The longer day by day, weekly, or monthly intervals are a top notch time to emerge as aware about method problems that are common among group contributors and to discover what needs a

follow up individual hassle fixing session. I had several people of a crew that determined that that that they had a cast off in getting monetary critiques from the finance branch if you need to set up their advertising and advertising and marketing and technique pitch decks. Once that changed into diagnosed as a technique hassle, I emerge as able to de-bottleneck it with the resource of the use of assigning all requests to undergo one liaison in the finance branch. The barometers have to have their private cadence as properly, whether or not or not every day or weekly, and people aren't updates at the group's usual performance however as an opportunity on a fixed's power. Are they satisfied, sad, worn-out, indignant? Start with three easy questions for the first barometer and get comments from the group if exclusive subjects need to be considered at the same time as assessing the fitness of the crew.

The first questions can definitely be associated to a few Es:

• Endorsement: Do you sense you and/or your group individuals are aligned at the identical goal and equal time limits?

• Execution: Are the strategies in location effective to collect consequences? What doesn't work?

• Excitement: Do you feel you have got had been given the useful resource of management? Do you currently experience the tactics in location allow for paintings/existence stability?

2. Individual hassle solving: Each group member will subsequently hit a roadblock. Once diagnosed in the each day or weekly meeting, it wants to be solved together with the group manager. Roadblocks are not something you tell a team member to transport determine out for themselves, due to the fact proof has proven this is while the maximum essential drop in productivity takes place. Let's additionally be smooth, that 'contemporary' roadblocks are dealt with the equal manner inside the feel that the supervisor lets in manual the revolutionary dressmaker in the right path but doesn't continuously remedy the hassle in detail. Once the roadblock seems to be

circumvented, and there may be a present day path beforehand, then ensure to have a look at up preceding to the subsequent assembly to look if the corporation member modified into a achievement on this new course. Don't deliver yourself the risk to be disappointed. It is probably your fault as manager in case you are surprised that the paintings grow to be now not finished. The function of the manager in desired and in this man or woman trouble fixing is as SUPPORT. Please think about this feature in that way in case you need to preserve your group participants on course with out destroying their creativity or encroaching on their autonomy. Here are some hints of the exchange when trouble solving:

o 1) Identify the problem in a SMART manner (particular, measurable, actionable, relevant, and properly timed)

o 2) Don't resolve the problem. Support the organization member to maintain product/mission ownership

o 3) Encourage failure. It's adequate not to clearly resolve the problem sooner or later of the problem fixing session. Encourage the group member to attempt a few element and in the event that they find some other roadblock to carry it up for each specific comply with up trouble solving consultation.

o 4) If truely at a stand-even though, use root motive analysis. If neither you nor the product proprietor recognize what to do next, then write out the four Ws and H (what, whilst, in which, why, and how), or draw a fishbone diagram beginning with the problem and breaking it up into all its components. Simple tool to choose out out the idea purpose.

*To study the necessities of trouble solving, see the Concise Reads Problem Solving guide.

3. Performance metrics and visible boards: If responsibilities are long, and via prolonged I recommend weeks or months, then as a group supervisor you'll need to set up metrics which might be measured with each group replace and feature a seen board created. These days this may be a part of a dashboard or cloud based totally visual tool.

Performance metrics are unique to the task. For instance, if the crew aim is to boom client satisfaction, then one metric can be satisfaction based on weekly survey, or # of customer lawsuits, or # of merchandise lower lower back in step with week. If the mission is particular to a group member, then it is able to be patron satisfaction in line with crew member. The performance board offers the supervisor and importantly the organization a visible photograph of methods close to the organization or enterprise members are to their respective and collective desires. You can continuously undergo in thoughts the overall universal overall performance board as a flight time table. Things change all of the time, you can have delays or cancelled flights, and this wants to be available and visually easy to examine. As stated in advance, maximum of the PM equipment include a Kanban board. Explore the device you currently use. If you don't use one, take a minute to explore the severa notable system to be had on the facet of asana, wrike, trello, basecamp, or jira.

THE FEEDBACK CYCLE

Feedback is a brilliant middle a part of a manager's method. Many managers recoil at having to provide remarks. Some due to altruistic motives together with now not looking to hurt their team member's emotions. Others due to the truth they will no longer like working with their organization member and dread spending 1-on-1 time.

First, comments is a -manner street. No one is right, and that is a exceptional possibility for the supervisor to get feedback. Feedback sessions are not a corporation mechanism to make humans deeply reflect on their options. The motive is genuinely to decorate productivity of a group and has been tested to gain this. Targeted remarks facilitates assemble consider, encourages skill improvement, and leads to a higher functioning organization--consequently extra effective. In this phase, we'll research three key attributes to a fulfillment comments.

1. Have the right mind-set entering into

2. Appropriately conduct the comments consultation

three. Build an surroundings that encourages greater comments.

Feedback is practiced similar to taking a weekly barometer due to the truth they every simply improve productiveness ultimately considering glad people are efficient human beings (Theory Y of manage).

Approach to Feedback: First, as a reminder from the preceding segment, the feature of a manager is to useful useful resource. How you method remarks, similar to the way you set up your team kickoff defines whether or not or not the comments instructions will yield something or is probably an utter waste of time for each events. You want to:

Recognize the alternative birthday celebration for his or her strengths to date. This isn't always a praise sandwich. You have to handiest communicate about their strengths. It's been verified that the marginal growth in productiveness from growing one's strengths is severa orders of significance better than from growing one's weaknesses. So for the sake of productivity, interest on how strengths may be advanced.

Be prepared to talk about strategies their strength may be developed similarly. Constructive complaint based totally on a electricity can be properly obtained.

Ask them what they want to boom their strengths similarly, and the way you may help them. It is on your great interest to help your group members, but they don't assume that except you explicitly ask how it is which you or all and sundry else on the organization can guide them.

Ask what they would love to decorate on. If it is a weakness, then u.S.A. Beneficial guidelines that have helped you inside the past or be a part of them with someone who can assist. It's excellent enough to indicate on weaknesses from a social viewpoint as it builds believe, however it isn't a few detail you care approximately stepping into because it obtained't affect productivity as a good deal.

Conducting the feedback consultation: first it is an extroverted trait that many introverts overlook, and this is to start with social niceties. Feedback sessions are extremely annoying particularly in case you haven't built a trust dating yet. That is why it's miles critical to ask them approximately themselves, and take a look at a bit approximately them. Talk approximately the climate or the current statistics, and then ask "Shall we begin with the feedback?". This smooth intro to the comments periods will positioned the team member at ease and they will less likely be shielding whilst you speak about the observations you have of their strengths and the manner they might enhance.

Side be conscious: Some companies take transport of as actual with in being brutally sincere. They say such things as transparency and truth will cause improved common standard performance. That's proper, however for the untrained supervisor, it gives them sufficient of a leash to be their real egocentric, impatient, and rude selves. Giving feedback is a informed characteristic. So pay attention to me, begin with the niceties. You are handling people, no longer impassive robots. Then while you've set up take delivery of as real with, you may get to the reality or said less considerably, to the idea purpose of a hassle.

During the feedback session:

a.   Listen! Taking an internet page out of Buddhism and professional treatment, it seems that one of the simplest methods to alleviate someone's inner suffering, frustrations, and poor feelings is definitely truly to pay interest. Listening is so powerful, which you'll see the institution member visibly greater snug once you've allow them to talk. Listening implies energetic listening, so in case you play on the side of your cellphone or takes notes at a few level inside the conversation, then all you're doing is growth the strain stage and decrease the opportunities the group member may be receptive to comments.

b.   Provide high-quality 1-2 honest observations: No you will be capable of listen to extra than 1-2 criticisms in a unmarried sitting. The magic range that triggers an emotional response is usually 3 areas to enhance on. Stay with 1-2 observations, and make certain they are honest. We all get induced thru the slightest remark, and I've heard managers say "I experience consisting of you don't seem involved or as enthusiastic as extraordinary business enterprise individuals". That is a horrible element to say, because it's far a mirrored photograph of the manager greater than it's far of the group member. It moreover isn't an actionable declaration. How are they going to 'seem' greater excited. Instead if they absolutely aren't excited, then a higher query is "I need to make certain everyone is satisfied with the paintings they're doing. How do you experience, and is there some thing I can do to get your entire guide?". If the latter query is requested, then you can display if the employee is absolutely excited or not and what movement to take to restore it. They can be excited, but the way they appearance or speak prompted the supervisor in a negative manner. Keep emotions out of the remarks consultation, and consciousness on sincere observations.

c.   Maintain a supportive tone: As you're discussing techniques their productivity may be superior or their strengths evolved, they may say some issue that you've already coached them on. In that instance, you may be brought on to transport from a supportive tone to an emotional one and blurt out "We already discussed this!". That assertion would possibly as properly surrender the communique. By paying attention to that you are emotional, the organization member will not want to have interaction with you and their productivity will not improve. Remember, your approach is to make sure all and sundry is doing their extraordinary art work to the incredible of their abilities.

The best comments consultation will consequently be hooked up in the following format:

i.   Ask to start the feedback consultation.

ii.   Lead with an honest assertion (1-2 most).

iii.   Explain the impact of that remark on the group, purchaser, or productivity.

iv.   Explain what it's miles that you want to advantage. Better team conversation, better productiveness.

v.   Ask what their comments is for you or the mission.

vi.   Suggest a few solutions and interact in high-quality speak.

Creating a culture of comments: to virtually make remarks second nature on your manipulate fashion and part of the organizational values, you'll want to reflect onconsideration on feedback as a help device to institution individuals and to internalize this radical concept that remarks is not about correcting the person but approximately improving the institution's overall performance.

In that feel you're finding faults in the technique and correcting them so honestly anyone can do their fantastic paintings to the first rate in their abilities. This additionally means that comments isn't always meant for the lousy performers however for all of us.

Everyone receives remarks.

That manner, whilst someone is called in for feedback, they do now not method it in a awful manner if you want to defeat the cause of feedback. Lastly, and most significantly, to create a way of life of comments is to ALWAYS ASSUME THE BEST OF INTENTIONS.

This is right advice for any communication, continually assume the notable of intentions. That manner, nothing you say will come off as horrible or trite.

We stay in a society in which all people is harmless till examined responsible, and because of the reality that 'motive' might be very difficult to expose, you better take delivery of as genuine with every group member is innocent and your interest is to assist them in any manner to decorate their conduct, productiveness, or verbal exchange.

Real anecdote: I as soon as had a more youthful MBA graduate be part of our group. Bright more youthful man or woman, but quality 26 years vintage. We took anybody out for a fun institution event, and that they made the mistake of eating too much. What they did next become no longer whatever brief of stunning within the organization worldwide however popular for a more youthful person jut presently turning into a member of the team of workers. They slurred and swayed and had their finger pointing at humans the complete night. The subsequent day, I had a comments session with them, mentioning their strengths in building relationships with the team. I cited my remark of the preceding night, and the way that in all chance impacted their gift and future relationships with the team. I then counseled them what I preferred, which changed into for stronger team relationships for higher collaboration. I paused (for effect). I then requested for the younger person's feedback. They defined that it changed into now not their purpose to harm relationships, that they preference this doesn't get them fired due to the truth they in truth just like the system and want to do the pleasant they may. I then engaged with the younger individual to find strategies to prevent this conduct from taking location in the destiny and methods to enhance the relationships in the team proper now. We agreed on the subsequent steps, and I asked if it became pinnacle enough to satisfy all over again in every week and note how what improvement has been made. They left feeling supported, and after apologizing to the institution, we soon determined a powerful and beneficial business enterprise member. I used my function as a supportive platform and assumed they had the exceptional intentions. After all, our frontal cortex splendid slightly finished developing by using way of 26 anyhow, however despite the fact that--professionally this may have price them their method someplace else and a set would possibly have out of location one its maximum collaborative contributors. Note, that their age became now not factored in. Statistically, it's just more likely a extra younger character can be receiving this comments consultation.

PERFORMANCE COACHING

While remarks is a static component in time, education is non-forestall. The goal of powerful schooling is to enhance performance. Similar to athletic education, there can be an detail of motivational education, however management coaches skip a step past that. They use specific observations, energetic listening, and thoughtful questioning to manual their employer participants to understand extremely good techniques they may be capable of enhance their normal performance. In this phase, we'll have a have a look at a framework for education periods in addition to discover ways to respect how the famous Socrates technique of thinking allows promote self-discovery inside the organization member.

How it differs from feedback: We've formerly observed out that in feedback durations, the manager first asks permission, then stocks an announcement and the effect to the organisation, pauses to accumulate comments from the crew member, after which starts offevolved offevolved brainstorming for feasible answers. Coaching is an extended comments consultation in that it takes place over an extended term with the motive of improving widespread ordinary performance and institution alignment and execution.

Let's check an example with the simple education framework.

Share An Observation: A manager observes that a collection member is sluggish to perform desires inside the path of the day while surrounded with one-of-a-type institution human beings but in the middle of the night sends emails with finished paintings. The manager stocks this observation with the organization member.

Manager: John, I've discovered which you are tons less powerful during the day however at night time when you are on my own you accomplish the desires of the day.

Use The Socrates Method Of Questioning: The supervisor then asks the institution member a series of questions in response to the institution member's solutions. For example:

Manager: John, do you pick operating at night time in preference to in the course of the day?

John: Yes I may additionally, however I'm genuinely more worn-out at night time time, and I'm afraid I can also additionally additionally make a mistake.

Manager: Why are you tired at night time?

John: Because I spend the higher part of the day assisting others with their art work

Manager: Do you find out that due to the reality you assist others with their paintings, you have got little time to complete your private art work?

John: Yes, but I apprehend I can always get to it after hours and I don't need to seem like I'm now not a crew player.

Manager: I count on helping others is a wonderful great to have, however how are we able to alternate the work surroundings so it does no longer prevent you from completing your paintings? I anticipate your

144

records is beneficial to the institution, however I moreover do not want you to art work time past law, so allow's find out a few element that works for each person.

John: I discover that once I'm interrupted at a few stage in the day, it takes me longer to perform my obligations. Maybe if I become interrupted lots much less frequently?

Manager: Are the interruptions for similar motives or are they one-of-a-kind?

John: Most are for the same cause.

Brainstorm An Action Experiment: The supervisor then makes certain to complete the training session with a course of motion. Similar to a unique feedback consultation, the intent is to guide the institution member and to technique the training training assuming the group member has the great of intentions. It is critical to have the proper attitude at the same time as education.

Manager: Do you determined you may be capable to finish your responsibilities inside the path of the day if we scheduled interruptions to a particular time of day?

John: Yes, and additionally if we had a conversation tool so wonderful organization members ought to see my answers to a previously asked query then that would appreciably lessen the interruptions.

Manager: Ok, that looks like a plan. What did you have got in thoughts?

John: Maybe we may additionally want to use Slack or a few special messaging platform, and I can also want to answer questions first rate amongst eight-10 am every morning?

Manager: That looks as if an check we can attempt. Let's revisit how that works after setting it in region for per week.

The above scenario is custom designed from the right GROW framework utilized in fortune 500 businesses. GROW stands for Goal (independent statement), Reality (lively listening and thinking), Options (brainstorming solutions), and Way beforehand (decide on an movement plan and comply with up conversation).

Socratic Paradox: Socrates, the historic Greek Philosopher, favored to test the Oracle of Delphi's announcement that he is the wisest man alive. Thus, he went to all of the high-quality professionals in Athens and requested them a query which they answered. He then observed up with next questions till subsequently each expert reached a element in which they didn't have an answer. At that element it is stated that he virtually believed he is the wisest guy alive because of the fact as he stated "I recognize that I apprehend not anything". What is thrilling about Socrates is that he certainly wasn't an expert in something. Literally, not whatever! He wasn't a Leonardo Da Vinci or a polymath. However, he end up clever due to the fact he knew that he knew now not whatever. It is that understanding that makes it great to examine Socrates ask question after question to specialists, information complete nicely that he does now not possess any answers, and for the simplest purpose of pushing the expert to without a doubt articulate their role and thru that gain a better know-how of themselves.

I factor out the Socratic Paradox, as it reinforces the location of the teach. As a manager and leader, you may often at times no longer have any answers or answers and need to method the training session with observations best.

That is the way it must be. It is the approach of energetic listening and thinking, all inside the spirit of assist, on the manner to help the institution member discover the concept motive of any declaration.

Just like Socrates, you can apprehend not anything about some thing and even though be an powerful teach.

Powerful notion, I apprehend. Just don't sell it on your boss that you recognize noting.

TEAM DYNAMICS

Now which you're an professional in the fundamentals of person comments and schooling for group participants. It is time to connect this to the wider company dynamics. In this concise section, we'll study identifying the common techniques groups underperform and appreciating that like feedback and schooling, this calls for an movement plan to get the crew aligned in its desires, and able to executing on these goals.

The first step in powerful crew dynamics is accumulating nameless remarks in the shape of a survey.

If you google 'enterprise dynamics survey' you'll see hundreds of various surveys, some handiest 5 questions prolonged, others 50 questions prolonged. Each spark off is a question asking to rate a specific group function or a assertion asking to price how an lousy lot a group members has the identical opinion or disagrees. Here is a very smooth group dynamic survey with a rating from 0 for surely disagree to five for absolutely agree:

1.   The enterprise is aligned in their goals and function thoroughly scoped the hassle and the manner ahead.

2. Each member of the crew is privy to and recognize their position.

three. Team contributors discover help from every distinct to complete their art work.

four. Team people are cushty raising issues or presenting their critiques in open communication.

5. Leadership is supportive and is actively worried in supporting the group obtain their goals.

6. The team is strong in identifying roadblocks early on.

7. The group executes its responsibilities in an organized and nicely timed style.

eight. Team individuals experience they are having a outstanding effect and that their artwork can also have a exquisite impact.

nine. The crew has techniques in vicinity to save you burnout and sell professional and personal lifestyles stability.

A not unusual surrender end result from those organization dynamic surveys is terrible alignment from the start of the group engagement. Poor alignment on scope and role results in siloed paintings, more common roadblocks, and repetitive paintings. Poor alignment together with lack of open communique, and burnout from imbalanced priorities consequences in poor execution of supposed dreams. That is why, the majority of effective crew dynamics begin with proper alignment that is placed through the group dynamics survey.

We found how effective barometers can be for small business enterprise productiveness. This is even more critical with larger corporations, and you may keep in mind a group survey as a larger, less not unusual, and additional comprehensive company barometer that looks at how individuals art work collectively in vicinity of the way people enjoy regarding their very very very own artwork surroundings.

Although apparent, it need to be stated. The outcomes of the institution dynamics survey need to be shared with the organization to brainstorm advantageous solutions moving beforehand. The supervisor need to no longer maintain those outcomes to themselves with the reason of creating unilateral adjustments.

1.   Greet Each Other Enthusiastically – Make an Effort!

Send out a happy, notable greeting, and most of the time you'll get lower back a cheerful, powerful greeting.

– Zig Ziglar

Daily, we rush to work in reality oblivious of the truth that there are human beings around. Even if we be aware them we wave an impersonal 'Hi' that is determined with the aid of a plastic smile. What if you worked in an workplace in that you had been the only worker? Can you visualise this type of scenario? Do you keep in mind Will Smith's movie 'The Legend', wherein the complete human race besides him can be wiped out and he finally ends up having a canine as his sole associate on the complete planet? Oh boy! If fine that have been to seem, you could recognize how lots you bypass over this morning ritual, which we frequently engage in a thoughtless manner. Aren't we lucky that we are running with such loads of people, some of whom we have to hold in mind friends? We take every different as a right! It is excessive time we favored each unique at paintings. Learning to greet every different enthusiastically may be a exceptional manner no longer handiest to start the day each day but moreover for building a exceptional paintings way of life inside the complete enterprise business enterprise.

2. Smile!

If no longer something else, the smile clearly distinguishes us from animals. Wear a smile to your face. It will make you enjoy cushty due to the neurological symptoms it sends your thoughts and it's going to make you a pleasant, approachable individual and everything else will examine. You should additionally apprehend while you smile it's far hard for someone not to grin decrease again at you. This all over again is due to how your thoughts is confused and due to what's called reflect neurons. We can write a entire e-book on reflect neurons and the characteristic it performs in animals and people but that is virtually beyond the scope of this e-book. Just to maintain matters easy, reflect neurons assist us look at new subjects by using imitating what we see, it bypasses our aware mind to make the mastering available. When you study a person smile, the mirror neurons are fired, you immediately respond even if you do not recognize the opposite character, you seize your self smiling midway, and make a aware choice to alternate the response. Have you noticed, on occasion whilst you are taking walks at the streets, you smile at a person mistaking him or her in your pal or an acquaintance? They smile again as well making you wonder whether or now not or no longer you surely apprehend them in any other case they couldn't have smiled lower lower lower back, proper? It's all a part of the thoughts circuitry so higher take benefit of it.

3.   Don't Think What's in a Name!

Even even though Shakespeare says, "What's in a name? That which we call a rose with the aid of a few specific call might probable scent as candy." you'll no longer want to do that at paintings or for that depend everywhere else if you want to strike a excellent relationship with a person. There isn't something in the route of a person's heart than one's name and you need to discover ways to leverage that correctly. Yes, use the decision of the person often whilst you're having a conversation with someone. This is what first rate communicators do. You ought to make the alternative person experience critical with out a particular efforts really by using manner of the usage of their name regularly to your verbal exchange.

4. Celebrate Birthdays

For a few uncommon cause, many people do not percentage with each person which encompass the team participants that they will be celebrating their birthday even on the correct day. They hold all of it hush-hush however deep internal, secretly preference that a person inside the team 'in some way' famous it out and wonder them with a gift or a party. When no longer some thing like that occurs, they pass lower back home feeling miserable and maximum seemingly telling themselves, "I am feeling depressing and I don't apprehend why!" What is the surprise? This is maximum human beings! If that have been to be the case, then why don't you are making it a habit to create, replace and keep a listing of birthdays of your team individuals? That isn't always everything - create a completely unique birthday ritual you can look at for each birthday – a easy however significant birthday celebration. How else can you've got an terrific time the gift of each one-of-a-kind in case you are not going to have a excellent time birthdays of the crew humans? Let that ritual now not be smearing of cake at the faces of each special observed via using 'endure-face' selfies to be published in social media for heaven's sake!

5. Celebrate Festivals

Festivals provide you with a purpose for birthday party and in India we're proficient with such quite a few fairs so take benefit of it too. Living in a various society like India, we ought to deliver out a completely strong message of concord not quality to the whole employer but moreover to the arena at huge through celebrating all the gala's with identical verve and vibe. Engage each person inside the practise whilst you are celebrating the ones festivals no matter their spiritual or language affiliations.

6. Wall of Fame

Display images of folks who did a high-quality interest at numerous degrees it can be some thing from consistency in assembly closing dates, attending client goals correctly, going out of the way to help first rate company individuals, and so forth. For some human beings, most of these gadgets come very definitely at the same time as others need to be stimulated and stimulated. When you apprehend individuals who do it genuinely via your Wall of Fame, others who want motivation and idea will grade by grade show involvement. You will complain an awful lot a lot much less that human beings are not displaying any private involvement. Dominos Pizzas has a few component along those lines, it skills well-known man or woman performers of their pizza stores. JewelOne capabilities their pinnacle earnings human beings of their Jewellery stores. Most of the arena-elegance companies have some aspect comparable for recognising the specific contributions of their employees. If you do now not have your Wall of Fame or some factor similar, set it up right away.

7.   Put in Place a Working Reward System

Setting up a praise machine or a 'elements' scheme is every special manner of recognising the achievements of your crew contributors. If you have got already got one, make sure that those elements rely! Many agencies take the initiative of putting in region this form of reward machine however on the surrender of the day, the factors gained via commendable efforts do now not rely for something. What is the use of having a rewards device if the elements do no longer rely for some thing? How do you expect the crew members to be stimulated with such an unrewarding, worthwhile device? Points scheme works inside the framework of 'micro-incentives', which offers people small doses of fun enjoy, firing the Mesolimbic Pathway or the Reward Pathway every time the points are scored and make the organization perform under usually inspired u . S . A .. If you want some thing you could connect with at once, do not forget the social media likes, it works below the same concept of 'micro-incentives'. However, while you positioned into effect this tool on your business business enterprise, you will additionally need to attention on making these elements rely for a few component for all your attempt to provide sustained effects.

eight.   A Positive Feedback a Day

Make it a factor to percent one super feedback to as a minimum one character each day and be real even as doing so! One of the presuppositions of NLP says we understand systems which can be inside us in others. Are you able to choose out many nicely topics in others? If positive, then you definately sincerely must recognize it's miles viable at the way to recognize those proper subjects in others only because of the fact you keep the ones systems inner you already. In different terms, what you select out in others is genuinely actual of you too. Start spotting right subjects in others and apprehend your self better. The identical is real of all those terrible and nasty belongings you word in others. Do you have got severa extremely good matters to word and percent with others or is all of it terrible belongings you observe in others? Initially, it will appearance very synthetic to inform someone a few factor awesome you study in them if you aren't used to it. However, if you do this often, you becomes an increasing number of adept in noticing suitable matters spherical you and you may be able to try this very virtually.

nine.   Create a Positive Feedback Calendar

Mark someone for each day on your workplace-calendar and allow the entire department or group send out extraordinary comments to the character marked for the day through e mail, SMS, WhatsApp or any other written layout so they might treasure it as a memento and pass all over again to it at a destiny date each time they want to revel in correct. Don't you discovered each one will eagerly watch for their day to pay attention what others have to say approximately them?

10.   Spot Recognition

We have spot exceptional, spot-correction, spot-approvals, why not spot-reputation? If you find out some thing appropriate in others, inform them instant without suspending. In fact it's far the maximum natural way to reply, we've got one way or the other misplaced it at our workplaces. It is excessive time we delivered returned this herbal behaviour to our artwork places so we can reap the blessings.

eleven.   Make Others Feel
Important

We are residing in a subculture of self-
importance and right here is an invite with
the intention to create a 'tradition of making
others enjoy vital' simply so whilst you depart
someone you go away them with an raising
experience. Organisations hold forth about
giving clients elevating enjoy with each
interaction, why most effective 'charity' need
to begin at domestic, why now not making
humans experience important and giving
them elevating revel in begin at home, giving
every different within the enterprise that
revel in? Most human beings regrettably
depart someone worn-out out, annoyed and
indignant via our unthoughtful phrases and
movements.

12.   Time for Treats

Pool coins to your department just so the
crew can take itself out for small treats like
ice cream treats, movie treats or wonderful
such similar treats. Many humans say their
university days have been the happiest and

you can be announcing the identical. And, one reason why college days had been so memorable is due to the fact you knew the manner to experience clean subjects in lifestyles and also you usually had some issue to have an wonderful time. You can emulate the same or at least a fraction of that at paintings.

thirteen.   Bring and Share

Organise 'deliver and proportion' luncheon sports as speedy as in a month or at the least as quickly as in three months. It doesn't fee you any coins or any special arrangements however this little interest that brings laughter and cheers will do a global of suitable for your crew. Absolutely harmless hobby, enforce it right away. Years in the past, I joined a smallish software program application organization with really round 40 normal humans then, which have become the time the company become beginning to develop and it have become in 2004 simply few years before the onset of the incredible monetary recession. I become heading the Content Development organization that factor and everyone, which means that all the departments stopped for lunch at the same time and we used to have lunch together and I am no longer exaggerating. Don't expect it is not feasible, we had been doing it every day, and it constantly felt like a large circle of relatives meal every day. We waited for each extraordinary to enroll in and people commonly controlled to wrap up matters, organise matters so they'll be a part of the agency. Lunch containers had been handed round, meals modified into shared and we pulled every other's leg, teased every exceptional, laughed loads and had a rejuvenating lunch. We had been no longer taking hours for lunch, we took forty to forty five minutes and that have become suitable enough. However, topics did alternate as the employer grew; human beings started out shifting out for lunch at considered one of a type instances but we nonetheless had lunch in companies but in smaller companies. Even if it is not feasible for us to perform a little problem like that daily, we're able to really paintings a few thing out along these strains at the least as soon as in a month.

14.   Monthly Themes

Celebrate numerous issues every month. One of the reasons why coming to artwork is dull is due to the fact we do paint a completely intense photograph about the art work place and tell ourselves that there is no room for amusing at work. This needn't be the case. Celebrate exciting subjects every month with a view to upload amusing at place of business. These topics can be very large and insightful. You can even run contests for growing with thrilling monthly undertaking subjects.

15.   Skill Inventory

Create 'who is right at what' stock on non-paintings related areas of interest and display it in a few place without a doubt so crew individuals can appoint their skills and specific skills every time desired and suitable. By doing this you may be capable of find out people's capabilities and additionally provide them a platform to market it their abilties. This is taken into consideration certainly one of learning the strengths of humans with whom we are walking.

sixteen.   Talent Evenings

Organise expertise evenings to encourage group members who've numerous abilties. You might be amazed to analyze the way gifted humans are and however you probably did no longer apprehend such abilities existed amidst you until the kind of platform have grow to be created for them. When we were greater youthful, we took factor in such a whole lot of competitions and activities, received prizes, were satisfied with our abilties but as we grew up, our priorities changed and we forgot to experience proud. We actually kicked such competencies out of our lives or absolutely let it die a herbal death. When you create such structures, you may permit human beings get associated with themselves and it's going to rejuvenate them. A suitable manner to get your group energised.

17.   Family Days

Given the fact that I created Family Gaga Family Enrichment Seminars for Married Couples (visit www.Familygaga.In for extra information and order your replica of my e book Fun on the Fly – 100 Interesting Ways to Have Fun with Your Family), you ought to be amazed if I do now not endorse this as one manner of creating a nice art work life-style. Of route, we do the entirety for our circle of relatives or as a minimum we are pronouncing so. If that is the case then if they're not a part of the show then there can be a few element incorrect. Often corporations painstakingly make a number of efforts to make everyone within the crew sense like circle of relatives. Here, it is amazing apt that we get to meet and have interaction with the actual families of our organization individuals. Organise own family get-togethers as a minimum as soon as a 365 days to facilitate this.

18.   Quote People

Yes, quote humans however my invitation is a touch one-of-a-kind right proper here. Identify a first rate quote that suits every enterprise member and post it at the noticeboard on the aspect of the choice of the man or woman inside the following format:

You can see people's eyes swell with tears when they see their 'existence quote' and this may make the individual even extra committed. Like the Feedback Calendar, you could set apart a day for each member inside the group for quoting people. Depending on your group period, you can tailor this interest.

19.   Employee of the Month Award

Nothing new approximately this! It is an age vintage exercise. If you do now not have this going already, then proper now installation employee of the month awards. Most corporations have this exercise - you have to not make it into a trifling ritual however manipulate it meaningfully. Give precise enough reasons for the nominations and for the final options.

20.   Business Innovation Brainstorming Sessions (BIBS)

Have as quickly as in a month Business Innovation Brainstorming Sessions (BIBS) but do now not motive them to proper into a formal meeting – motive them to into informal schooling. Let people take turns to moderate the ones conferences. You can be able to come up with progressive mind, merchandise and obligations that would take the organization to the following diploma.

21.   Encourage New Initiatives

We want human beings to be involved and be proactive but we thwart all new duties, what a contradiction between what we are announcing and do! Encouraging personal duties will robotically elicit personal involvement and it's miles contagious. With time, you may be able to see a incredible initiative spirit rising inside your organisation commercial enterprise enterprise. We want to observe from Google right right right here. You need to be aware that Google has been ranked thru Fortune due to the fact the "Best Company to Work For" in the US over five instances and severa instances in extraordinary worldwide locations too in conjunction with India. You need to have heard approximately "Google's 20% Rule," which changed into implemented in 2000. The enterprise encourages its personnel to spend 20% in their artwork time on some thing they like. Even despite the fact that there are debates whether or not this 20% rule is actually determined, whether or not or now not it's far 20% or one hundred twenty%, whether or not or no longer or not the employees have time to spare for such sports activities amidst their work strain and so on, what we can not deny is the truth that Google's pinnacle products which consist of Gmail it is used global (besides China) become in fact a factor assignment of one of the Google engineers named Paul Buchheit who worked for almost and 1/2 years in this, which modified into one in every of his dream responsibilities. Similarly, some other flagship made from Google, AdSense is also a fruit of Google's 20% rule. If you observed Google is a cutting-edge-day business enterprise to try such guidelines for the number one time, you're wrong. This has been a policy observed with the aid of 3M as early as 1948 out of which unintentional merchandise together with, the well-known 'Post-it Notes' and 'Trizact' one of the flagship abrasives of 3M have been invented. Do you believe you studied you may truly get the tremendous from your personnel with the aid of smothering them with art work and by means of using making them slog past their jogging hours? Such an technique will handiest depart you with personnel who are bodily and mentally burnt-out and no modern juice will secrete from such tired out employees. What are you doing in a first-rate way for your corporation to inspire innovation and private tasks?

22.　　　　　　Be Available

When the organization people want some time, make yourself available. This is relevant for the group chief similarly to the institution humans. If you are a manager or a team lead, then you definitely have a in addition responsibility of making your self to be had. Do no longer faux you are a tremendous-essential person and meeting you should now not be that clean. No depend wide variety what function you maintain in your company, no person is crucial. You can be the supervisor or the organization lead however there can be not some thing wrong in making people reporting to you, feel crucial. I actually have seen every sorts of managers; one which makes their institution contributors experience like scum and additionally managers who make their institution individuals experience critical after every assembly along with her or him. I genuinely have furthermore seen the cooperation degree of the crew members in both times. It shouldn't be hard in an effort to bet who gets higher cooperation. Managers who reliable and recognized their institution members were not most effective famous within the businesses however they could gain their goals more resultseasily than the others. If you want to get, increase and keep the involvement degree of your institution participants, you have to inspire human beings in preference to trying to steer them through your authority, strength and function. When you're inspiring, the weight of having to make people do what you need them to do is proper away off your shoulders. People may be more than inclined to participate and get involved. How without hassle to be had are you? What is your control version – do you have an effect on or encourage?

23.   Regular Meetings

Hold normal month-to-month conferences to connect to your group besides the same old enterprise assessment meetings and the P&L meetings. Let each person revel in they are heard, and that there is constantly a platform to voice out one's evaluations and views. If you do now not provide them that platform, they may vent out within the wrong places. Most importantly, let no person experience they were factor included or ignored in those meetings.

24.   Have an Eye to Spot Goodness

Be quick and organized to become aware of the good things that humans do or accomplish no matter how small. In fact, at the same time as you switch out to be perceptive of the little topics, that are often omitted and ignored as insignificant and allow them to recognize you have got were given taken observe or that such things have no longer lengthy past disregarded, you can no longer awesome take people by means of way of the use of surprise however you will additionally earn a unique vicinity of their coronary heart. This approach will in reality spread an air of positivity round you.

Remember, a while ago we had been talking about 'Spot Recognition'? It is feasible for you to try this first-rate when you have a eager eye to spot easy appropriate subjects that people do.

25.   Straight Talk

Whenever you have a bad remarks or something to criticise, share it immediately with the individual involved and do not talk about it inside the again in their another time to others. Nothing else comes as 'acid rain' as this one close to destroying even the little positivity that is already there inside an employer.

26.   Positive Gossiping

Are you thinking whether or not or no longer there can be anything referred to as top notch gossiping due to the truth gossiping by means of definition is lousy or poor? Yes, there can be and I would really like to hold the oxymoron 'top notch gossiping'. Be disciplined to stay faraway from calumny. If the group people have some component to share approximately someone or a few other group to others in their absence, allow it best be pinnacle subjects about them. Positive gossiping have to be encouraged as it has many benefits and a remarkable impact at work place. There cannot be a better manner to inspire your crew individuals not right now than through excellent gossiping. You need to area your self within the footwear of the alternative character to understand what wonderful benefits effective gossiping have to bring to the floor. When I changed into sharing this concept to someone, the person have end up asking, "What is the gain of talking suitable subjects about others of their absence, what benefit does it deliver to the table?" Further dialogue unravelled that this person is of the opinion that horrible or bad matters will spread faster than effective topics. For some purpose, we have a tendency to assume or we are made to trust terrible facts and negativity travels quicker than excellent news - we also can even quote many examples to show our stand but that isn't real. News genuinely travels, each awesome and lousy. Both awful statistics and super records are there all of the time. What you hobby on is what you be aware extra. If you recognition upon the terrible subjects you may get to hear many awful subjects due to the reality that's what you be conscious greater. If you consciousness on wonderful subjects you could notice there may be severa pleasant news spherical us. Even superb subjects tour speedy and this is how we listen about suitable ingesting locations, unique films, top provider corporations and such an entire lot of various real topics which can be around us. I assume no extra clarification is needed here to similarly offer an motive for the advantages this approach is possibly to bring on your crew and on your agency. Make this a way of life at your paintings vicinity and you could attain unlimited blessings at the longer term.

27.   Let People Celebrate their Success Stories

What is wrong in celebrating one's very own success tales? Allow human beings to have fun their private successes in a healthy manner with out branding it as 'boasting'. We want pretty some fantastic memories round us to live inside the superb bubble. Why have to we revel in intimidated or enjoy 'now not so outstanding' to place it euphemistically even as someone is captivated with their achievement? Why do you need to be prompted fine with the aid of the usage of using studying books on exquisite wondering in which the writer boasts of his or her fantastic successes in every awesome web page of the ebook, during the book? Do you no longer need to concentrate such success memories and high-quality episodes of human beings round you? Actually, you can connect to tales which can be near domestic with out difficulty than to the memories of some unknown authors. Sharing one's achievement recollections ought to come to be a normal aspect at your workplace, a few trouble part of your paintings way of existence. If people can go to Alcoholic Anonymous agencies and distinctive such assist corporations to stay inspired to stay at the right song regardless of something their supported desires have been why we cannot do the equal with our non-public success tales. Do we not want to be on target with our pursuit of creating a excessive exceptional paintings subculture and a instead successful crew?

28.　　　　　　　Celebrate the Successes of diverse Departments too

It is surprising how people can draw very strong barriers spherical themselves, thinking about the wrong motives. It is sad that we do now not have the potential to have an excellent time the fulfillment of various departments. Is this actual or now not? We need to have opposition out of doors the enterprise and now not internal. How can we win whilst departments test every distinctive as competition? There is a few trouble grossly wrong if this kind of situation need to be successful to your business organisation. I even have seen this unhappy plight in all sorts of agencies and in academic establishments, in factories and groups in the company enterprise. Team, if that is what you're then why reduce lower back its boundaries most effective on your department. For whom the other departments are working and towards what cause the alternative departments are transferring? It is however every other no-brainer that you may win as an agency best through manner of helping each distinct and simply now not via stopping each one-of-a-kind or with the aid of way of pointing arms at each extraordinary.

29.   Positive Communication

Let all communications take a effective take a look at, even the worst comments you want to percentage should be toward undertaking a excessive quality surrender cease result. It need to not be to region down someone or to embarrass a person. If you use this usually of thumb, all the communications will now not only become tremendously powerful but you can also get better responses for your communique. This does not suggest you want to continuously reward humans or overlook about the regions that want correction. Positive communique never approach turning a blind eye to errors.

30.   Jokes Corner

Set aside noticeboard vicinity for 'comic story of the day' and ensure that this region is used without fail. There are outstanding techniques to move about it. Let humans pin funny prices and jokes on this area. To get topics started, take turns to submit in this place. Soon you can see people coming beforehand to put up here and the hobby diploma in the jokes nook developing over a duration. The wall location you pick out out for the Jokes Corner ought to be consequences available to humans and it want to be located in spots that people frequently go to without fail every day. It is probably inside the lobby place, next to water dispenser or the canteen the front.

31.   Listen Before You Speak

Speak simplest on the identical time as you're willing to pay interest. Most people do not have the potential to pay attention. We pass spherical in a 'non-listening mode,' which results in a large style of issues inside departments and among departments. By inculcating the dependancy of listening you may result in a massive transformation interior your organization. The HODs, Managers and Team Leaders have to be prepared to be aware of folks who document to them and vice versa.

32.   Art of Active Listening Training

If you be conscious that humans do no longer have the functionality to concentrate or in the event that they lack this best or skill inner your corporation or branch, you want to educate them. This potential might be learnt with the beneficial resource of subjecting humans to formal artwork of lively listening training programs. I absolutely have conceived a complete-day workshop on the "Art of Active Listening" which permits human beings to emerge as greater open, receptive and independent listeners. This is one region in which people do now not even comprehend their need to decorate. Every Manager, Team Leader and HR professional need to get hold of the 'Art of Active Listening' education in advance than they take in obligations and leadership roles.

33.   Do now not Take Home Office-artwork

When my partner favored to join an company to take in a system, one of the topics I advised her is to decide now not to deliver domestic art work from place of business. This is what I advised her, "As lots as the business organization might not can help you peel our potatoes for the duration of the jogging hours, we also can not allow place of business paintings to invade our own family time or your private time. Try to offer your two hundred% at art work, however when you go away art work, you go away the work." This is an crucial desire all of us need to make. If no longer, we come to be stealing our non-public time for the want of assembly workplace deadlines or for finishing place of job duties. Staying once more at work longer than the stipulated hours want to not be considered self-discipline. It is rather a limitation as regards to time control skills and making plans skills of the character and terrible resource management competencies of the supervisor if they'll be overloading the personnel. This isn't a seasoned-employee idea. If your personnel do not have a healthy, balanced life-style then you definately genuinely and your bottom traces are the ones for you to get affected. Never allow human beings to take domestic paintings as an alternative deliver them exact enough guide and schooling to end up inexperienced although it way sending them for powerful time manage training programs. This could additionally talk a brilliant deal about your delegation and aid control abilities. Month-cease stress is what I pay interest from nearly all companies. If month-give up stress is an occasional state of affairs, it need to no longer be a hassle, however if it's miles taking vicinity each month, then you definately really need to revisit your methods, take right enough steps and corrective measures.

34. Be Realistic with Your Deadlines and Targets

Be sensible while setting goals and final dates. You can set hard desires however it have to never be smothering dreams and closing dates. In continuation to what I shared in the earlier section approximately taking domestic place of job-paintings, the issues is probably prevented through taking a sensible method. To get the excellent out in their companies it is ordinary to set tough cut-off dates and targets. However, you want to be cautious right here now not to get your crew demotivated. Sense of fulfillment will hold your institution advocated in desire to creating them continuously live in a enjoy of inadequacy. If they're constantly falling quick of their goals and cut-off dates, the institution will start shopping for the concept that they may be an insufficient institution and as quick as that takes place, even if you lessen the workload thru 50% the subsequent month they'll discover techniques and method to fall short. On the alternative hand, at the least initially, if the dreams set are effortlessly capacity, it'll deliver your institution the self belief they are an green institution. They will very personal that identity and might now not need to lose it and at this factor on the identical time as you gradually growth the objectives and invite them to carry out greater correctly, you can see them going for walks at their pinnacle of the line stages. The institution building capabilities of the managers and team leaders are crucial here. Train the leaders for your company in order that they apprehend a way to construct and keep prevailing groups.

35.   Avoid Scapegoating

Overload nobody just because they are succesful. In each company and in every enterprise there might be one or more folks that take in greater work and responsibilities than the others. In most of the agencies they're taken gain of and in some conditions lamentably even exploited. First, be sensitive to such institution members, feed them nicely with tough desires so that their internal wants to accomplish subjects are met and at the identical time, do now not overload them or reason them to clean desires for last minute or pressing assignments. Most importantly, make certain your rate determinations deliver them sincere returns every in terms of their pay hikes and in terms of promotions. If they're now not appeared at the right time, they may withdraw and flow into to passive resistance. They may want to in the long run even emerge as as underperforming people of the organization. As a pacesetter, it is your responsibility to groom your crew individuals and float them to the following level. When you comprehend humans for his or her particular efforts and skills, allow the other institution individuals recognize why precisely they were mentioned or promoted simply so the rest of the enterprise does now not see you as being partial. Every employee, even the underperforming ones assume they may be doing their exceptional and that they're being handled unfairly.